EVIL AND
A GOOD
GOD

EVIL AND
A GOOD
GOD

BRUCE R. REICHENBACH

1907

New York
FORDHAM UNIVERSITY PRESS
1982

BJ
1481
.R44
1982

Printed in the United States of America

For
ROBERT

whose world of good and evil
still lies before him.
May he never return evil for evil,
but always love and do
the good.

ACKNOWLEDGMENTS

I want to thank Augsburg College for granting a sabbatical for the spring term of 1979 and the National Endowment for the Humanities for a 1978 Summer Seminar Stipend. These provided both time and resources to enable me to make substantial progress on the manuscript. The editors of the following journals have kindly consented to allow me to reprint materials from my articles which were published in their journals. "Natural Evils and Natural Laws: A Theodicy for Natural Evil," *International Philosophical Quarterly* 16 (June 1976), 179–96, is revised and included in Chapter 5. Chapters 4 and 6 incorporate revised parts of my article "Must God Create the Best Possible World?" *International Philosophical Quarterly* 19 (June 1979), 203–12. "The Deductive Argument from Evil," *Sophia* 20 (April 1981), 25–42; "The Inductive Argument from Evil," *American Philosophical Quarterly* 17, No. 3 (July 1980), 221–27; and "Why Is God Good?" *The Journal of Religion*, 60 (Jan. 1980), 51–66, appear partly revised as Chapters 1, 2, and 7, respectively.

Contents

Preface

Horror and fascination mingle as we watch old films of war. Rows of men, defaced and dehumanized by gas masks, charge out of the trenches to meet uncertain fate. The front of the LST lowers and battle-clad marines storm the beaches, leaping their fallen comrades in their rush to establish a critical beachhead. Soldiers aim their flamethrowers to incinerate the enemy concealed in the island caves. Kamikaze planes wing a straight and deadly path to the aircraft carrier's tower, while tracer bullets pave the lighted way. Children emerge from a napalmed village, their ragged clothes and brown bodies burned and charred. Gaunt faces atop emaciated bodies peer from behind barbed wire fences.

The tragedy is not all history; it is found daily in the papers. Bodies lie like cordwood rotting in the hot Guyana jungle, victims of religious brainwashing and utopian delusion. Blindfolded, arms pinioned behind their backs, men give a final lurch and then slump as bullets rip these enemies of the revolution. Thieves knock the elderly to the ground, grab the purse and run.

Horror and fascination mingle as we watch disasters unfold on the theater screen. Great earthquakes rock the metropolis, shaking buildings, while thousands, screaming, crowd the streets. Like a towering inferno a skyscraper is engulfed in a crescendo of fire, flames driving the occupants ever higher. Rows of triangular white teeth sparkle as a mechanical shark sweeps clean the beaches of New England.

But these Hollywood fantasies can scarcely approach

the fury and terror of reality. Two flaming Boeing 747s tangle in Tenerife, their survivors struggling to escape the exploding jet fuel. Cracks skim across the countryside and white hillsides testify to the tens of thousands who died in the collapse of their adobe houses in the great Guatemalan earthquake. Rows of concrete pads are evidence that houses once stood before the tornado littered the landscape with matchsticks. The silent cries of the parents whose thirteen-year-old boy dropped dead in the back seat of their car from a heart attack bear witness to the sudden unexpectedness of death.

In what follows we will not concern ourselves with the fascination, though this in itself would provide an interesting topic: why do people flock to fires or snatch up magazines which headline tragedy in living color? What attracts people to the catastrophic or to become eager spectators of the suffering? Rather are we concerned with the horror—not the horror per se, but with the relation of the horror to the theistic world view. These horrors are evils, and evil is often held to establish the falsity of the theistic world view. Evil is believed to be either logically inconsistent with the existence of a good, omnipotent, omniscient, loving, personal deity, or else of such a great amount, prevalence, and variety that it is improbable that God exists. Were either of these true, and consequently were it possible to show that the theistic world view is false or probably false, this would be a significant intellectual and practical conclusion.

In our study we will examine this atheological claim, in both its deductive (Chapter 1) and inductive (Chapter 2) forms. In Chapters 3 to 5 we will present a theodicy for evil, attempting to show that a morally sufficient reason can be given for the evil present in our world. In the final three chapters we will consider issues which are related to

the problem of evil. In particular, Chapter 6 will deal with
the question whether God must create the best possible
world, whereas Chapters 7 and 8 will consider the properties of goodness and omnipotence which usually are assumed to characterize God.

MORAL AND NATURAL EVIL

In what follows we shall employ a traditional philosophical distinction between two kinds of evil: moral and natural. Moral evil is all the instances of pain and suffering—
physical and mental—and all states of affairs significantly
disadvantageous to the organism which are caused by actions for which human agents can be held morally blameworthy. It is important to note that not all pain, suffering,
or dysfunction caused by human agents is to be classified
as moral evil. It is restricted to evils for which human beings can be held morally culpable, where the agent inten-
tionally and/or knowingly performed a morally wrong
action.[1] Suffering which is caused by agents who did not
intend acts morally blameworthy, as when one accidently
strikes and injures with one's car a child who dashed into
the street between parked cars, or when one damages a
pitcher's eye with a hard line drive, is to be classified as
an instance of natural evil.

Natural evil is all the instances of pain and suffering—
physical and mental—and all states of affairs significantly
disadvantageous to the organism which are caused by actions for which human agents cannot be held morally
blameworthy. A host of causes of natural evils can be enumerated: non-human causes like cancerous cells, viruses,
defective genes; natural calamities like floods, drought,
famine, and tornadoes; creatures of nature such as mosqui-
toes, tsetse flies, parasites, carnivores, and sharks; and man

himself. Both human and non-human causes are involved.

It is obvious that we are classifying evils not by reference to any inherent or derived quality which the evil itself
might possess. Such a method of classification would seem
impossible to implement. Rather we are classifying evils
with reference to their causes, and more especially with
reference to the moral implications of the causal acts. Further, since we are taking these two classes to be mutually
exclusive and totally exhaustive, it might be even more
appropriate to term the two types of evil morally caused
evil and non–morally caused evil. However, though these
are more accurate and hence preferable designations, we
shall adopt "moral evil" and "natural evil" since they are
widely used in the literature. We shall treat each of these
kinds of evil in turn in Chapters 4 and 5.

THE SIGNIFICANCE OF EVIL

Some might think that the theist, in attempting to provide
a justification for evil, fails to appreciate fully the extent,
force, and severity of evil and suffering. The theist who
holds that God is using evil to fulfill consciously his own
purposes in the perfecting of the human person gives the
appearance of trying to turn evil into good.

But our endeavor to provide a morally sufficient reason
for pain, suffering, and dysfunction should not be seen as
an attempt to turn evil into good or to deny the reality of
evil. That there is a morally sufficient reason for evil does
not affect the essential character of evil: evil remains evil.
That taking an antirabies injection has substantive medi-
cinal value to an exposed person does not make the shot
and its results any less painful. What the presentation of a
morally sufficient reason does is establish that the existence and quantity of evil in the world do not entail the

denial of or make improbable the existence, goodness, knowledge, or power of God. Indeed, the fact that the theist feels impelled to present defenses and theodicies implies that he takes seriously the existence of pain and suffering. He acknowledges the awfulness of man's inhumanity to man; he empathizes with those who struggle against natural evils and seeks some reason behind the apparently inexplicable suffering. He treats both moral and natural evils as realities which must be reconciled with his theistic beliefs.

Furthermore, the adoption of a defense or theodicy does not leave the theist immobile in the world. That pain, suffering, and dysfunction can be reconciled with God's existence, power, knowledge, and goodness does not entail that we should stand by while others suffer. As we shall argue, God is active in the world to prevent evil and reduce suffering. Indeed, were God not active, there would be exponentially greater evil than currently exists. One way in which God is active is through human persons. The theist who holds that there is a morally sufficient reason for evil is consistent in working to prevent or alleviate those evils; that evil or the possibility of it can be justified does not entail that it must be accepted or tolerated.

Finally, the view presented below might or might not be of value in helping an individual deal with particular experienced evils. The problems one encounters vis-à-vis evils may be intellectual in nature, or they may more greatly reflect one's emotional state than what one reasonably holds. C. S. Lewis has suggested one way to view faith—namely, as holding on to what our reason has decided to be true in spite of emotions and passions.[2] We do not always operate according to the dictates of our reason. Though we know something to be true, and have strong evidence in support of it, circumstances can so affect our emotions and passions that we forget what we have reasonably concluded and instead side with the opposite opinion. Lewis provides the following example:

> My reason is perfectly convinced by good evidence that anaesthetics do not smother me and that properly trained surgeons do not start operating until I am unconscious. But that does not alter the fact that when they have me down on the table and clap their horrible mask over my face, a mere childish panic begins inside me. I start thinking I am going to choke, and I am afraid they will start cutting me up before I am properly under. In other words, I lose my faith in anaesthetics. It is not reason that is taking away my faith: on the contrary, my faith is based on reason. It is my imagination and emotions. The battle is between faith and reason on the one side and emotion and imagination on the other.[3]

So understood, what we have to say below might have little to say to our emotions but much to say to our reason. It is directed to helping our reason come to a rational conclusion regarding the question whether one who acknowledges the reality and significance of evil is required to abandon his belief in God's existence, goodness, omniscience, or omnipotence. In this respect it addresses the person who is struggling with a belief in God because of his encounter with or increased awareness of the evil prevalent in our world. But insofar as we are to bring our emotions and passions into line with our reason, the theodicy developed can speak meaningfully to our emotions as well.

BRUCE R. REICHENBACH

Augsburg College
January 1982

NOTES

1. This definition of moral evil does not require us to determine what constitutes the standard of right and wrong action, only to assert that there is such a standard or set of standards available. Of course, to ascertain in any particular case of evil whether it is an instance of moral or natural evil would require determination of the standard—at least in part—according to which persons are held morally culpable or excluded from culpability.

2. C. S. Lewis, *Mere Christianity* (New York: Macmillan, 1952), p. 123.

3. Lewis, p. 122.

EVIL AND
A GOOD
GOD

1

The Deductive Argument from Evil

THE SO-CALLED PROBLEM OF EVIL can be posed in both an inductive and a deductive form. In his inductive argument from evil the atheologian[1] contends that the variety and profusion of evil found in our world, though not logically inconsistent with God's existence, make it improbable or unlikely that God exists. For example, Hume writes,

> . . . [A]s [God's] goodness is not antecedently established, but must be inferred from the phenomena, there can be no grounds for such an inference, while there are so many ills in the universe, and while these ills might so easily have been remedied. . . . The bad appearances . . . may be compatible with such attributes as you suppose. But surely they can never prove these attributes. . . . However consistent the world may be . . . with the idea of such a Deity, it can never afford us an inference concerning his existence. The consistency is not absolutely denied, only the inference.[2]

We shall consider this argument in the next chapter.

In his deductive argument from evil, the atheologian maintains that the existence of evil per se is logically inconsistent with the existence of a good, omnipotent, omniscient God. Flew writes, "The issue is whether to assert at the same time first that there is an infinitely good God, second that he is an all-powerful Creator, and third that there are evils in his universe, is to contradict yourself."[3] Flew affirms that it is.

Whereas in the inductive argument the amount, intensity, and variety of evils actually occurring in the world are critical to the case, in that the greater the amount, the stronger the intensity, the more abundant the variety, the more unlikely it is that a good, omnipotent, omniscient God exists, in the deductive form this is irrelevant. So long as there is any evil whatsoever, there exists a contradiction between it and God's existence. Here extensive enumeration of evils has no bearing on the case; the mere existence of one evil is sufficient to generate the contradiction.

Since the formulation of the alleged contradiction is fairly standard among atheologians and variations are of relatively minor importance, and since J. L. Mackie presents a clear deductive argument, we will utilize his presentation as representative of the atheologian's position. In an oft-referred-to passage Mackie reiterates the charge of logical inconsistency.

> I think, however, that a more telling criticism can be made by way of the traditional problem of evil. Here it can be shown not that religious beliefs lack rational support, but that they are positively irrational, that the several parts of the essential theological doctrine are inconsistent with one another. . . .[4]

Mackie asserts that there exists a contradiction between:

(1) God is omnipotent.
(2) God is wholly good.
(3) Evil exists.

He admits, along with more recent writers following his line of attack,[5] that these propositions do not yield an explicit contradiction, i.e., a contradiction where one proposition is the denial or negation of one of the other propositions; to obtain an explicit contradiction other propositions must be added, propositions which must be either necessary truths or propositions accepted as true by the theist as part of his essential core beliefs. The former propositions will express "some quasi-logical rules connecting the terms 'good,' 'evil' and 'omnipotent,' "[6] and at least one of these "must be an analytic, ethical principle if the contradiction or incompatibility that is claimed to exist, is to be a logical one involving a self-contradiction."[7]

Mackie suggests the following:

(4) Good is opposed to evil, in such a way that a good thing always eliminates evil as far as it can.
(5) There are no limits to what an omnipotent thing can do.

From these he concludes

(6) ∴ A good omnipotent thing eliminates evil completely. [4 & 5]
(7) ∴ God eliminates evil completely. [1, 2, & 6]
(8) ∴ God eliminates evil completely and evil exists. [3 & 7]

In short, employing the necessary truths (4) and (5), a contradiction between (3) and (7) can be generated.

Is Mackie's argument sound? (1) and (2) seem unexceptional in that they are generally affirmed as theistic core beliefs, and (3) is true by experience. (6), (7), and (8) validly follow, which leaves propositions (4) and (5). Taking (5) first, Mackie himself admits that it perhaps presents an inadequate analysis of omnipotence. There are "limits" to what an omnipotent being can do in the sense that an omnipotent being cannot bring about a state of affairs whose description contains or entails a contradiction; it cannot bring about logically necessary truths or the logically impossible, not because it lacks some ability, but because logically necessary truths and the logically impossible cannot be brought about. The former hold true in all possible worlds and the latter in none. But this "limit" would not reasonably be held to count against a being's being omnipotent.[8] Indeed, the latter "limit" is critical to the atheologian's own case. Unless it is inconsistent with God's nature to do that which involves or entails a contradiction, the problem of evil is no problem at all, for in that case the presence of a contradiction between God's goodness and the existence of evil would not mean that one would have to be sacrificed. God could allow or even bring about evil and still be good. Thus we must amend (5) to read

> (5a) An omnipotent thing can bring about any contingent state of affairs, the description of which does not contain or entail a contradiction.

Likewise (4) is inadequate. For one thing, the existence of a good person is compatible with the existence of evil if that person did not know about the existence of that evil.[9] That is, a good person can be expected to eliminate only the evil about which he knows. Thus (4) should read

> (4a) A good thing eliminates every evil it knows about as far as it can,

and correspondingly (1) must be amended to read

> (1a) God is omnipotent and omniscient.

(1a) can be affirmed as a theistic core belief; what about (4a)?

The "it can" in (4a) remains unclear. Mackie takes it to mean simply "is able." But so understood (4a) is not true. A good being might refuse to eliminate an evil it is able to remove and be justified in its refusal. In particular, it would be justified in not removing an evil when the removal would bring about a greater evil or prevent a greater good. It is not a question of its ability to remove the evil; it can remove it—but it would not be good if, in doing so, more evil is brought about. For example, I could remove a failure from one of my students' papers—a grade which he surely would perceive to be an evil—and replace it with a higher grade. But to do so might bring about more evil or at least prevent a higher good. The student might then continue to bank on my good will for passing grades and not learn the material. Thus, I would not be good if I arbitrarily removed it and my refusal to remove the evil (the failure) would be consistent with my goodness. Again, a physician could remove severe but short-lived pain by giving strong doses of morphine, but one who did this would (in some cases) not be good because, though he removed the pain in question, he brought about a greater evil (supposing addiction to occur). If one is to be a good person, one will eliminate evils only where the elimination will not reduce the overall good or increase the overall evil. In the last case the physician will have to decide whether to administer this pain killer in light of the severity of the patient's pain, his life expectancy, etc.—i.e., calculating the total good that can be produced by his action. Thus we have

(4b) A good thing eliminates every evil that it knows about and can eliminate without bringing about a greater evil or lesser good.

Suppose we grant the necessary truth of (4b) and (5a); does (6) follow? What does follow is not (6) but

(6a) A good, omnipotent thing eliminates every evil that it knows about and can eliminate without bringing about a greater evil or lesser good.

But (6a), along with (1a) and (2), does not entail (7). What follows is

(7a) God eliminates every evil he knows about and can eliminate without bringing about a greater evil or lesser good.

But then (8) does not follow, for in a world with a good, omnipotent, and omniscient God there might indeed be evil—evil whose elimination would require bringing about a greater evil or producing a lesser good. For the atheologian to make his case for (8) he must rescue (7), and to rescue (7) he must introduce another proposition, namely,

> (9) An omnipotent and omniscient thing can eliminate every evil state of affairs without losing a greater good or producing a greater evil.[10]

If (9) is true, it follows from (9), (1a), (2), and (6a) that (7) is true, and thus the contradiction found in (8) can be generated. But is proposition (9) true? It is not a proposition to which the theist must consent because it is a member of his theistic core beliefs. Thus, if it is to be true, (9) must be necessarily true. Is (9) necessarily true?

Alvin Plantinga argues that not only is (9) not necessarily true, it is not even true.

> Suppose that evil E is *included in* some good state of affairs that outweighs it. That is, suppose there is some good state of affairs G so related to E that it is impossible that G obtain or be actual and E fail to obtain. . . . Then not even an omnipotent being could eliminate E without eliminating G. But *are* there any cases where a good state of affairs includes, in this sense, an evil that it outweighs?[11]

Plantinga goes on to suggest several such cases: a person is heroic in the face of a bad situation, or another shows moral courage in bearing pain magnificently. Since heroism and bearing pain magnificently are goods, but goods which do not obtain unless there be evil states of affairs, we have cases where a good state of affairs includes an evil that it outweighs.

IS EVIL EVER NECESSARY TO THE GOOD?

H. J. McCloskey, adopting an atheological stance, professes to be unconvinced by the kinds of instances suggested by the theist. The theist, he contends, has not established that the instances in which good states of affairs include evils that they outweigh are such that God could not have done something to eliminate or prevent those evils without creating a greater evil or losing a greater good. There are, he suggests, three possible types of instances or cases to which the theist could appeal. Let us consider his critique of each in turn.

First, there is the possible case where the evil is a *means* to achieving a particular good. Consider the example of the surgeon who brings about evil for his patient in order to eliminate a particular evil of another sort. The surgeon cannot remove the diseased organ or repair the rupture without creating an incision and bringing about its accompanying pain. But the intent of the operation is a greater good G, to which the incision E required by the surgery is a necessary means.

But, McCloskey argues, this appeal to evil as a means to good is not an instance where G is so related to E that it is impossible that G obtain and E fail to obtain.

> We countenance the use of evil means only when good means are not available. . . . An omnipotent God is able to achieve all the goods directly, without using means, which in the human situation require on occasion evil means, and this because of the limitations of human power.[12]

That is, as finite humans we are restricted to these pain-causing means because of our limited power and knowledge. But God as omniscient would know that using such and such means to achieve a certain end would bring about pain (evil) and as omnipotent could bring about the end directly without using those means. Thus, cases where evil means are necessary to achieve a good end do not provide legitimate counter-examples to (9).

McCloskey's argument here depends upon the thesis that God is able to achieve all goods directly, without using means or secondary causes. But this premiss, as we shall argue in more detail shortly, is suspect. For example, consider the good state of affairs: P freely chooses to act bravely. Now God cannot bring about this good state of affairs directly, for to do so would contradict the freedom with which P is choosing to act bravely.

However, suppose we leave aside descriptions of free states of affairs. Then McCloskey's argument here against these counter-cases seems correct, provided that the means envisioned in the particular instances are only empirically and not logically or metaphysically necessary for the end. If the latter were the case, then God's omnipotence would be an irrelevant consideration in any given case, for if God cannot do that which involves or entails a contradiction, then God cannot bring about the end without bringing about the means which are logically or metaphysically necessary to realizing that end. Whether there are cases of this sort is left undetermined by McCloskey; the cases appealed to—for example, the case of the surgeon—are not of this kind.

However, even granting McCloskey's contention with regard to particular cases, his argument fails to show or establish that (9) is true. That it is logically possible for God to bring about *particular* ends directly without utilizing the evil-producing contingent means does not entail that, were he to do this in *every* case, the toti-resultant state of affairs would be better than the state of affairs which would result were God to allow the end to be produced by natural law-governed but evil-occasioning means. To assume that since the good end in each particular case can be achieved directly without utilizing evil-occasioning means, the whole is such that the ultimate good achieved by so eliminating all the evil-occasioning means is a greater good or that no greater evil has resulted—i.e, that (9) is true—is to commit the fallacy of composition. As we shall argue below, though it is logically possible that God operate a world by miracle (immediate divine intervention directly to achieve the ends), it does not follow that this would be a better state of affairs than where God allowed the end to be achieved by natural but evil-producing means. As we shall show in Chapter 5, worlds which are operated by divine miraculous intervention are substantially inferior to worlds operated by natural laws because it is impossible that there be moral agents in worlds operated by miracle. But a world in which there are moral agents choosing between good and evil and choosing a significant amount of moral good is superior to a world lacking moral agents and moral good and evil. Hence, though some particular evils can be prevented through the direct intervention of God to produce the ends, in worlds where this becomes the norm, where all ends are produced or at least all evil prevented in this fashion, a greater good (the existence of moral agents) is lost. But this runs counter to the contention of (9), according to which every evil must be eliminated or prevented without losing the greater good. Consequently, even were McCloskey's thesis that God could intervene to produce the particular end directly and thus eliminate the evil means involved true (in cases where the connection between means and ends is contingent), it would not be sufficient to establish the truth of (9).

The *second* kind of possible case is where evil is a *by-product* of securing the good or of the good itself. McCloskey asserts that what is required here is that the evil not merely happen to be a by-product of the good, but that it be "*logically* consequent on the goods or the means of achieving them."[13] That is, G entails E. [Plantinga's above refutation of (9) also seems to make the same requirement.] But this is not so; to refute (9) it is sufficient that the *possibility* of the evil be a logical consequent of the greater good. That is, should the possibility of there being evil be necessary to securing the good or to the good itself, and should the possibility be realized in actual evil, God cannot eliminate this evil (or even prevent the possibility of its being realized) without removing or eliminating the greater good. Indeed, apparently unrealized by McCloskey, his examples proceed precisely along this very line. The greater good which results in the world from free human persons' choosing a significant amount of moral good entails the possibility that these same free persons can choose to perform evil actions. It is not that they will perform evil acts; the evil is not logically consequent upon the good. Rather, what is entailed by the good is the possibility that they will perform evil acts. But should the possibility be realized, there is an evil which God cannot prevent without losing a greater good, which fact constitutes a refutation of the truth of (9). Similarly, the greater good which results in the world from free persons' choosing a significant amount of moral good entails the necessity of the regularity of natural laws and the consequent possibility that these sentient persons can experience natural evil. It is not that they will experience natural evil; their experiencing natural evil is not logically consequent upon the good. Rather what is entailed by the good is the possibility that they will experience natural evil. But should the possibility be realized, this is an evil which God cannot prevent without losing a greater good, which fact constitutes a refutation of the truth of (9).

McCloskey rejects this kind of case as a possible counter-case refuting (9) on two grounds: (a) an omnipotent being could prevent all physical evils, and (b) an omnipotent being could cause only those who will be morally good to come into being.[14]

On what grounds is (a) true? The only plausible ground is that an omnipotent and omniscient being can eliminate every evil state of affairs. But this would be to argue in a circle: (a) is true because (9) is true, and (9) is true because (a) is true.

(b) is more complex. The following argument might be given in support of (b).

(10) That the only free agents which come into being are those which, when they choose between doing good and doing evil, always choose the good, is a state of affairs the description of which does not contain or entail a contradiction.

(11) God as omnipotent can bring about all states of affairs the description of which does not contain or entail a contradiction. [1, 5a]

(12) ∴ God as omnipotent can bring it about that the only free agents which come into being are those which, when they choose between doing good and doing evil, always choose the good.

Before we consider (10–12), it is important to distinguish argument (10–12) from the following argument, with which it is easily confused.

(13) That free agents, when they choose between doing good and doing evil, always choose the good, is a state of affairs the description of which does not contain or entail a contradiction.

(11) God as omnipotent can bring about all states of affairs the description of which does not contain or entail a contradiction.

(14) ∴ God as omnipotent can bring it about that free agents, when they choose between doing good and doing evil, always choose the good.

According to (14) God himself brings it about that these free agents always choose the good. As such, he could guarantee that the only agents which exist which choose between good and evil are those which always choose the good. But such agents cannot rightly be called free agents, for their choices and actions are determined by God. A being cannot be said to be caused by another to freely choose to do the good. Hence, (14) contains a contradiction and does not describe a state of affairs one would expect an omnipotent being (or any being) to be able to bring about. That is, it is logically impossible for God to bring it about that *free* agents always freely choose to do the good.[15]

What is expected of God in (12) differs from (14) in that (12) affirms that God can cause to exist agents, all of whom freely always choose the good. In (12) God does not directly bring about the free agents' choices of good over evil. What he brings about is the existence of beings who themselves freely always choose the good. As such, (12) should be understood as asserting

> (15) God as omnipotent can bring about the existence of free agents which, when they choose between doing good and doing evil, always choose the good.

But though according to (15) it is possible that all the agents God creates always choose good when faced with a moral choice, it is also possible that these free agents sometimes or even always choose evil. In creating agents with free moral choice, God cannot guarantee that those persons will always choose to perform the right rather than the wrong. To provide such guarantees God would have to override individual agent freedom.

Consequently, the following seems to be the case in (12) understood as (15). God can bring about the existence of certain free persons, and it is possible that they will always choose the good; but God cannot bring it about that these persons will always choose the good freely, for this latter—(14)—is self-contradictory. But then though (*b*) understood as (15) be accepted as true, it neither refutes the counter-case to (9) nor establishes the necessary truth of (9). (9) claims that an omnipotent God can eliminate all evil from the world. But whether there is evil in the world does not depend solely upon God and his omnipotence but also upon free persons. God created free persons, and they might all always choose the good, or they might sometimes or always choose evil. Thus, though (10–12) be accepted as sound, it does not follow that if God exists and is omnipotent there will be no evil in the world or that he could eliminate all evil from the world. Of course, if (*b*) were understood as (14), this would refute the counter-case and establish the truth of (9), but as we have seen, (14) is false because it contains a contradiction.[16]

It might be replied that our argument has taken account only of God's omnipotence and not of his omniscience. God, as omniscient, can know all possible states of affairs and all possible persons, and can know what all possible individuals might freely choose in all circumstances, and can on the basis of this knowledge actualize only those individuals who he foreknew would always choose rightly when faced with moral choices. That is, (12) should not be understood as either (14) or (15), but as asserting that

(16) God as omniscient knows which agents, when they would choose between doing good and doing evil, always would choose the good, and as omnipotent can create only those agents.

From this it would follow that (*b*) is true and that (9), on the theist's own premises, is likewise true.

This reply leaves little doubt that the atheologian has the following model in mind. God knows all possible states of affairs, all possible individuals, and all compossible states of affairs and individuals, and on the basis of this knowledge can choose to actualize the compossible state of affairs in which no evil is committed or suffered. As the supreme dramatist all possible scenarios are known to him, and from these possible scenarios he chooses to actualize those characters who he foreknows will always act rightly. And since foreknowledge does not determine, the actions and choices of these characters remain free.

This model presupposes that God's knowledge includes propositions about what individuals would choose were conditions different from what in fact obtain or about choices made by possible individuals: i.e., that God's knowledge includes counterfactual conditionals of free will. This means that he knows states of affairs which not only will never occur, but which are the possible results of free choices which never were or will be made. But in what sense are counterfactuals about the free choices and acts of individuals and possible individuals matters of God's *knowledge*? To be part of his knowledge they must be true. But are counterfactual conditionals of free will true? They are not true by correspondence with any actual occurrence or state of affairs, for as counterfactuals there will be no actual occurrence or state of affairs so described. These choices will never be made by actually existing individuals, nor will the possible individuals ever exist in order to make them. Thus they are not simple matters of God's foreknowledge, for there is no actual choice or state of affairs for him to foreknow. Neither are they true in that they are the causally necessary results of non-subsequent conditions, for this is inconsistent with their being conditionals of free choice or action. Neither are they true in that they correspond with or follow from the possible person's character or intentions, for a "free agent may act out of character, or change his intentions, or fail to act on them at all."[17]

Insofar as he is not necessitated by his character, what he would have done remains indeterminate. In sum, it appears dubious that counterfactual conditionals about free acts of actual or possible agents can be true and hence could constitute part of God's knowledge. But without this dubious presupposition the atheologian's model collapses and his reply fails.

Contemporary analyses of counterfactuals do not require us to change this opinion. Some philosophers, following Robert Stalnaker, suggest that a counterfactual is true "if and only if its antecedent is impossible, or its consequent is true in the world most similar to the actual in which its antecedent is."[18] But this analysis fails to rescue the model in that it fails to show how these counterfactuals could be true and known by God in such a way that he could actualize a particular world based upon this knowledge. As here described, whether a counterfactual (excluding those whose antecedents are impossible) is true depends upon the actual world in respect to similarity of relevant states of affairs. But if counterfactuals of free choice are to be items of God's knowledge and if they are to be used in his selection of agents who always freely do the right, God must know them *before* (logically, if not temporally) there was an actual world *and before* he decided which possible world he would actualize. But he cannot know them before this since it is yet indeterminate which world will be actual and hence which contingent propositions and hence which counterfactuals will be true. To put it another way, there is a circularity underlying this model. The truth of these counterfactual conditionals depends upon there being a particular actual world, and which world is actual depends upon God's knowing all counterfactual conditionals and choosing to actualize that compossible set of beings which freely always choose the good (i.e., which world is actual depends upon the truth of the counterfactual conditionals).[19] (16), then, must be rejected as expressing an impossible state of affairs.

In conclusion, there is no reason to think (*a*) true, that (*b*) understood as (14) or (16) is not impossible, or that (*b*) understood as (15) establishes (9). Thus the counter-cases against the necessary truth of (9) stand.

The *third* kind of case is that in which "certain goods are logically dependent on the existence of certain evils, [such] that without the evils the goods logically could not exist. . . . The goods cited here include benevolence, fortitude, sympathy, determination, industry, and the like."[20] McCloskey here has in mind the argument of Ninian Smart, who urges that certain virtues exist only in connection with evils like temptation, adversity, and competition. Heroism occurs in resisting temptations, courage in the face of difficulty, generosity in resisting self-interest, pride amid competition.[21] If man were wholly good, impervious to temptation, and incapable of being affected by difficulty or adversity, these virtues would be unrealizable. But these virtues are that to which we refer (in part) when we ascribe goodness to human persons. Accordingly, here we have a counter-case to (9) in which, without the existence of evils such as self-interest, temptation, difficulty, and adversity, the greater goods of courage, benevolence, and pride cannot exist.

McClosky disagrees. First, he argues that it is possible to develop these virtues apart from the *existence* of these evils; it is sufficient that the individual *think* that his friends are in need to evoke benevolence, that he *think* there is danger for him to show courage, that he *think* another suffers to show sympathy and concern. McCloskey answers his own objection, however, when he writes that "one could not get the concept of suffering without experience of it by oneself or someone else."[22] One can cry "Wolf!" only so many times when there really is no wolf before the cry ceases to evoke any response, and if there never were or could be wolves, could the cry even arise? Furthermore, the kind of world envisioned here is one based on deception. I think that another suffers or is in want and needs my help, but I merely *think* that this is the case; in fact the other suffers no ill at all. I think that something threatens my life, and call up the courage to face or endure it, but I only *think* that my life is threatened when in fact there is no threat. But now, though the envisioned evils are not real, another evil has taken their place: the evil of systematic deception. "But if the world is to be populated with imaginary evils of the kind needed to enable creatures to perform acts of the above specially good kinds [acts of forgiveness, courage, self-sacrifice, compassion, overcoming temptation], it would have to be a world in which creatures are generally and systematically deceived about the feelings of their fellows—in which the behavior of creatures generally and unavoidably belies their feelings and intentions. I suggest, in the tradition of Descartes, that it would be a morally wrong act of a creator to create such a deceptive world."[23] Finally, the connection between certain virtues and some evils is not empirical but logical. Whether or not one's perception of the evil is accurate, it is still the case that the virtue in question only has meaning in connection with the evil. One can understand what courage is only if one understands what danger and fear are, or what overcoming adversity is only if one understands what adversity is.

McCloskey's second objection appears more telling. He writes,

The value judgment involved is completely untenable. The goods concerned are not intrinsic goods; and their instrumental value is much less than is assumed in this argument. These facts become evident if we consider the human situation. We do not deem the goodness of the goods as being such as to justify artificially introducing evils into the world. Only a very evil husband would beat, torture, torment his wife, and ultimately kill her in order to develop such goods as fortitude, tolerance, kindness in the wife and compassion, sympathy and benevolence in her friends, parents, children and neighbors.[24]

It should be made clear what McCloskey's argument does and does not show. It does not show that the above-listed virtues are logically unconnected with corresponding evils, such that without these evils the goods are unrealizable. What it does question is whether these goods are sufficient to warrant their introduction (along with their corresponding evils). That is, are these goods such that G outweighs E? If in these cases G does not outweigh E, then these cases do not constitute counter-cases to (9). On the other hand, even were McCloskey's argument correct, it would not show that (9) is true or necessarily true. In short, McCloskey's argument functions solely as a refutation of a particular kind of counter-case.

In this limited capacity, does it succeed? The answer depends upon the truth of his contention that we do not deem the goodness of these goods as sufficient to justify artificially introducing evils into the world. But this, as a general truth, is false. Perhaps the most obvious case concerns athletics, where adversity, physical and mental hardship, even outright physical pain are introduced in order to generate pride of accomplishment, self-sacrifice to team interest, courage, and fortitude. The particular evils introduced to encourage development of the virtues are contingent, but the connection between the virtues and evil is necessary in that the virtues cannot be achieved without encountering adversity of some sort.

Of course, McCloskey is correct that it is not always justifiable to introduce evil to generate these virtues; or, perhaps better, some evils, were they introduced, would

outweigh the goods produced. War—which generates
many of the same virtues as athletics—is a case in point.
But to refute (9) it need not be argued that all evils which
in turn produce or provide occasion for the development
of certain virtues are justified. One needs only one case
where the introduction of evil is both required and justified. Our mention of athletics is a case in point.

McCloskey's final complaint that no significant moral
philosopher lists such virtues as courage, fortitude, mag-
nificence in bearing pain, and generosity in his list of intrinsic goods is beside the point. What is at issue is simply
whether here we have at least one case where G entails an
E which G outweighs. We have provided such a case. Thus,
though McCloskey's argument shows that this will not
justify all evils present in the world—which is really to
shift to the inductive argument—it does not refute the type
of counter-case to (9) here advanced, and hence fails to
rescue the deductive argument.

In short, the atheologian has not refuted the counter-
cases against the truth of (9). Of course, in the strict sense
the whole question of actual counter-cases is irrelevant to
disproving the *necessary* truth of (9). It is relevant to its
truth, but not to its necessity. The mere possibility—
which seems undeniable—that there is some G so related
to E that G outweighs E and it is impossible that G obtain
or be actual and E or possibly E fail to obtain would establish that (9) is not a *necessary* truth.

We may conclude, then, that the atheologian has not
shown that (9) is a necessary truth, and consequently
has not established that there is a contradiction—either implicit or explicit—between propositions 1a, 2, and 3. That
is, he has not shown that there is a logical incompatibility
between the claim that God exists and possesses the properties of omnipotence, omniscience, and goodness and the
affirmation that evil exists. Of course, that the atheologian

has not shown there is an incompatibility does not mean that there is not one; the required necessarily true principle might be lurking somewhere in the neighborhood. But it does show that, despite all the ballyhoo, the atheologian has not yet made his case, and it would seem that the burden of proof in this matter rests on the atheologian to prove his case that the propositions in question are inconsistent.

To complete the theist's case one should proceed further to show that the propositions in question are in fact logically consistent. To do this, i.e., to show that (1a) and (2) are compatible with (3), the theist must suggest a non-contradictory proposition (M) which, when added to (1a), (2), and (3), shows that (1a) and (2) are compatible with (3). For if (1a) and (2) are compatible with (3), given (M), (1a) and (2) are compatible with (3) simpliciter.

Further, (M) need not be true, known to be true, or even plausible; to establish consistency it need only be possible. However, though logically this is the case, yet as Swinburne notes, if "the assumptions which I make are clearly false, and if also it looks as if the existence of God is compatible with the existence of evil *only* given those assumptions, the formal proof of compatibility will lose much of interest."[25] To avoid what might appear to be logical gamesmanship, I believe it is important that the theist show that (M) is true or at the very least, given what we know about God and the world, plausible. That is, it is incumbent that the theist show that (M) not only is possible, but that there is good reason to think (M) is true as well.

In what follows I shall use the language of Nelson Pike and term (M) a morally sufficient reason for the existence of evil, where a "morally sufficient reason is a circumstance or condition which, when known, renders *blame*

(though, of course, not *responsibility*) for the action inappropriate."[26] I intend to suggest an adequate morally
sufficient reason for the existence of evil, one which, given
what we know about God and the world, is plausible and
seems true. Of course, even if I am unsuccessful in Chapters 3 through 5, this would not prove the atheologian's
case, for it must be remembered that he still has not shown
that there is an inconsistency. Failure of any particular (or
every) theodicy will not in itself rescue the atheologian's
argument. There is no necessity that God reveal all his
purposes to mankind—though in a revelatory religion it
is reasonable to expect that he might reveal some important
ones. Thus, even if any theodicy be defective, there exists
the possibility that God has another morally sufficient reason for evil.

Repeated failure by theists to provide a morally sufficient reason for evil might suggest that possibly such a
reason is not to be found. This in itself does not occasion
any difficulty with respect to the rationality of belief in
God if one already has independent grounds for knowing
the truth of (1a) and (2). If they are true, it would be
reasonable for the theist to reply that God must have a
morally sufficient reason for evil, though in fact we do not
know what it is.[27] It requires independent grounds, however, for knowing the truth of (1a) and (2). The atheologian presumably does not possess such grounds. Rather,
the incredible amount of suffering endured by men and
animals, the mass catastrophes, and the unjust distribution
of pain and suffering, coupled with the repeated failure
to discover a viable morally sufficient reason, will for him
constitute adequate grounds for denying God's existence
or his possession of traditionally ascribed properties. That
is, the amount and distribution of evil in the world, though
not incompatible with God's existence, make it unlikely

or improbable that God exists. We turn to this inductive argument from evil in the next chapter, and from there to the attempt to present an adequate morally sufficient reason for evil in Chapters 3 through 5.

NOTES

1. Individuals who present arguments to show that God does not exist or that it is unreasonable to believe that he exists can, parallel to natural theologians, be called natural atheologians.

2. David Hume, *Dialogues Concerning Natural Religion* (New York: Hafner, 1948), pp. 78, 73.

3. Antony Flew, *God and Philosophy* (London: Hutchinson, 1966), p. 48.

4. J. L. Mackie, "Evil and Omnipotence," *Mind* 64, No. 254 (1955), reprinted in Nelson Pike, ed., *God and Evil* (Englewood Cliffs, N.J.: Prentice-Hall, 1964), p. 46.

5. H. J. McCloskey, *God and Evil* (The Hague: Nijhoff, 1974), pp. 5–8.

6. Mackie, p. 47.

7. McCloskey, p. 6.

8. We will say more about this in Chapter 8, where we will take up a detailed study of omnipotence.

9. Alvin Plantinga, *God, Freedom, and Evil* (New York: Harper & Row, 1974), p. 18.

10. Plantinga, p. 22; McCloskey, pp. 70–77.

11. Plantinga, p. 22.

12. McCloskey, p. 72.

13. McCloskey, p. 73.

14. McCloskey, p. 74.

15. Since (14) is self-contradictory, the argument (13, 11, 14) must be unsound. (14) follows validly from (13) and (11), and (13) seems undeniably true. This leaves (11) as the questionable premiss, which means that (5a) provides an inadequate definition of omnipotence. In Chapter 8 we shall advance the following definition of omnipotence (which we shall likewise suggest is inadequate in that it is too broad) adopted from George Mavrodes, "Defining Omnipotence," *Philosophical Studies* 32 (1977), 199–200.

(C) A being x is omnipotent if and only if (1) it is capable of bringing about any contingent state of affairs (*a*) whose description does not contain or entail a contradiction, and (*b*) whose description does not exclude or entail the exclusion of x or any omnipotent agent from among those which may have brought about that state of affairs.

Using this definition, we might express (11) as follows:
(11a) God as omnipotent can bring about all states of affairs the description of which does not contain or entail a contradiction, or exclude or entail the exclusion of God from among those which may have brought about that state of affairs.

(13) must then be rewritten as

(13a) That free agents, when they choose between doing good and doing evil, always choose the good, is a state of affairs the description of which does not contain or entail a contradiction nor exclude or entail the exclusion of God from among those which may have brought about that state of affairs.

But then (13a) is false, for the state of affairs of free agents' always choosing the good necessarily excludes any other agent, including God, from bringing it about that they freely always choose the good.

Replacing (11) with (11a) in the argument (10–12) does not affect (10) in the same way as it affected (13). That is,

(10a) That the only free agents which come into being are those which, when they choose between doing good and doing evil, always choose the good, is a state of affairs the description of which does not contain or entail a contradiction, nor exclude or entail the exclusion of God from among those which may have brought about that state of affairs

seems to be true, such that the deduction of (12) from (10a) and (11a) is materially unaffected.

16. This argument is similar to that advanced by Alvin Plantinga in *God and Other Minds* (Ithaca: Cornell University Press, 1967), pp. 135–41.

17. Robert Adams, "Middle Knowledge and the Problem of Evil," *The American Philosophical Quarterly* 14, No. 2 (1977), 113.

18. Alvin Plantinga, *The Nature of Necessity* (London: Oxford University Press, 1974), p. 174.

19. A more detailed presentation of this argument can be found in Adams, 112–15.

20. McCloskey, p. 74.

21. Ninian Smart, "Omnipotence, Evil and Supermen," *Philosophy* 36, No. 137 (1961), reprinted in Nelson Pike, ed., *God and Evil*, pp. 105–106. See also Thomas Aquinas, *Summa contra Gentiles*, III, 71n6.

22. McCloskey, p. 75.

23. Richard Swinburne, "The Problem of Evil," in *Reason and Re-*

ligion, ed. Stuart C. Brown (Ithaca: Cornell University Press, 1977), p. 90.

    24. McCloskey, p. 75.

    25. Swinburne, p. 82.

    26. Nelson Pike, "Hume on Evil," *The Philosophical Review* 72, No. 2 (1963) reprinted in Nelson Pike, ed., *God and Evil*, p. 88.

    27. George Mavrodes, *Belief in God* (New York: Random House, 1970), p. 93.

2

The Inductive Argument
from Evil

REBUFFED WITH HIS DEDUCTIVE ARGUMENT, the atheologian often turns to the inductive argument from the existence of evil.[1] Rowe calls it "the evidential form of the problem of evil: the form of the problem which holds that the variety and profusion of evil in our world, although perhaps not logically inconsistent with the existence of [God], provides, nevertheless, *rational support* for the belief that the theistic God does not exist."[2] This echoes Hume's earlier comment: "However consistent the world may be . . . with the idea of such a Deity, it can never afford us an inference concerning his existence."[3] Or to put it another way, the pain and suffering which occur in our world make it unlikely or improbable that a God who is good, omnipotent, omniscient, loving, and personal exists.

How is this unlikelihood or improbability to be understood? Is there any way of formulating the inductive argument or improbability more precisely? Since atheologians have appealed to a standard theorem of probability calculus called Bayes' Theorem[4] elsewhere in philosophical theology—for example, to suggest that the teleological argument serves to make improbable rather than probable God's existence[5]—it is appropriate that we here employ Bayes' Theorem to reconstruct the atheologian's thesis that it is improbable that God exists given the amount of evil in the universe.

Bayes' Theorem can be formulated as follows, where

P(B/A) means the probability of B on (given that, with respect to) A.

$$P(B/A\&C) = \frac{P(B/A) \times P(C/A\&B)}{[P(B/A) \times P(C/A\&B)] + [P(\overline{B}/A) \times P(C/A\&\overline{B})]}$$

We can assign the following meanings to the above symbolism.

$P(B/A)$ = the *prior probability* that the original hypothesis is true, given the background evidence.

$P(\overline{B}/A)$ = the *prior probability* that the original hypothesis is false, given the background evidence.

$P(C/A\&B)$ = the probability that the effect will be observed, given that the hypothesis is true.

$P(C/A\&\overline{B})$ = the probability that the effect will be observed, given that the hypothesis is false.

$P(B/A\&C)$ = the probability that the hypothesis is true, given the background evidence and the fact that the effect is observed.

In applying this theorem to the problem of evil, I will restrict my formulation to the problem of natural evil, for the sake of simplicity. I believe that the evidential problem of evil could be formulated in terms of Bayes' Theorem for both moral and natural evil, but this broader formulation would only serve to complicate the issue while not strengthening the case for the atheologian. Further, the fact is that the atheologian's case frequently is constructed on the basis of natural evil.[6] The atheologian might develop his inductive argument along Bayesian lines ascribing the following meanings to the above symbolism.

$$P(G/N\&E) = \frac{P(G/N) \times P(E/N\&G)}{[P(G/N) \times P(E/N\&G)] + [P(\overline{G}/N) \times P(E/N\&\overline{G})]}$$

where

$P(G/N)$ = the probability that a personal, loving, omnipotent, omniscient, perfectly good God exists, given the furniture and structure of the world (including sentient creatures, insentient creatures, physical objects, and laws of nature, but *excluding* any morally sufficient reason, defense, or theodicy for evil, any construed evidence for God's existence, or evil).[7]

$P(\overline{G}/N)$ = the probability that a God as described above does not exist, given the furniture and structure of the world.

$P(E/N\&G)$ = the probability of there being 10^6 turps of natural evil (the amount of natural evil that exists in our world), given that the world described above obtains and the God described above exists.

$P(E/N\&\overline{G})$ = the probability of there being 10^6 turps of natural evil, given that the world described above obtains and the God described above does not exist.

$P(G/N\&E)$ = the probability that God as described above exists, given that the world described above obtains and there are 10^6 turps of natural evil in the world.

To begin, how do we determine the value of the *prior probabilities*, $P(G/N)$ and $P(\overline{G}/N)$? Two approaches, yielding different conclusions, might be suggested.

(1) The atheologian presumably holds that none of the traditional reasons advanced by the natural theologian suffices to establish the existence of God,[8] while the natural theologian, for his part, might well contend that some do succeed.[9] Thus, in terms of the total evidence available to both, neither would be willing to grant the other his respective claim regarding God's existence. In such a case, the atheologian might argue, it would be appropriate to assign a value of ½ to $P(G/N)$ and correspondingly to $P(\overline{G}/N)$.

If we assign a value of ½ to these *prior probabilities,* it follows that the value of P(G/N&E) will depend upon the relation of P(E/N&G) to P(E/N&$\overline{G}$). If P(E/N&G) < P(E/N&$\overline{G}$), then P(G/N&E) < ½; and if P(G/N&E) < ½, the atheologian has a prima facie case with respect to natural evil, i.e, the existence of an omnipotent, omniscient, good, and loving God is improbable. Indeed, the greater the disparity between the two probabilities in favor of P(E/N&$\overline{G}$), the more improbable God's existence is, prima facie. The atheologian's conclusion in (1), then, is that the natural evil in our world disconfirms—i.e., yields a value of less than ½—God's existence.

(2) A second, weaker approach would be to suggest that the value of P(G/N) is not important in the argument so long as it is neither 0 nor 1. What the atheologian wants to know is what the role of the natural evil occurring in our world is with respect to disconfirming God's existence. That is, does the amount of pain and suffering found in the world *tend to* disconfirm—i.e., make it *less probable* —that God exists? In order to focus specifically upon the role of evil, we want in effect to abstract from any other confirmatory or disconfirmatory evidence for God's existence. Thus, we can assign any *arbitrary* value to P(G/N), other than 0 or 1, that we choose. If we assign it an arbitrary value, the above argument regarding P(G/N&E) will still obtain, except that a weaker conclusion must be drawn. Whatever the value of the prior probabilities, if P(E/N&G) < P(E/N&$\overline{G}$), then the resulting value of P(G/N&E) will be less than the prior probability P(G/N). Thus the atheologian has a prima facie case with respect to existent natural evil, i.e., it makes belief in an omnipotent, omniscient, good, and loving personal God *less probable.* Indeed, the greater the disparity between the two probabilities in favor of P(E/N&$\overline{G}$), the less probable God's existence is, prima facie. The atheo-

logian's conclusion in (2), then, is that the natural evil found in the world *tends to disconfirm*—i.e., lessens the probability of—God's existence.

The difference between the two arguments is important and can easily be overlooked. Strictly speaking, it is (1) which is essential to the atheologian's case, for it is (1) and not (2) which serves to refute the thesis that God exists. Argument (2) might succeed inductively, and yet fail to show that God does not exist, for his existence might be assigned a high degree of prior probability based on other evidence. Only if the prior probability $P(G/N)$ were extremely low or if $P(E/N\&\overline{G})$ greatly exceeded $P(E/N\&G)$ could argument (2) be turned into an atheological inductive disproof of God's existence.

Is there a disparity between the value of $P(E/N\&G)$ and $P(E/N\&\overline{G})$? That there is such a disparity, the atheologian argues, is a result of what one would expect from an omnipotent, omniscient, good, and loving personal deity, for in the presence of such a deity one would anticipate that there would be less evil than would be the case without his activity. This is precisely what we expect regarding other good persons. We rely on good people to remove, prevent, or alleviate the natural evils which we encounter and which they are capable of affecting. Parents remove splinters, bind up cuts, relieve their children's hunger, provide shelter and clothing. The physician prescribes medicine to relieve pains and distresses. At the very least, we expect him, if he is good and knowledgeable, not to bring about more pain and suffering than we would have undergone had we not consulted him, and at best we expect that by his knowledge he can bring it about that we suffer no more or diminished pain by following his directions than we would by letting nature take its course. If there is generally less natural evil because of the activity of good persons with limited power than there would be were they not active for good, how much more can one expect that there would be less natural evil in the presence of a perfectly good and omnipotent personal deity than if the natural laws were simply allowed to run their course with respect to the furniture of the world?

For one thing, good, powerful persons are capable of intervening in the laws and activities of nature, such that by introducing new factors into the situation or removing present ones they can prevent the painful consequences of previous conditions. Might not God, in the same way, so intervene in the natural order as to prevent evil? This thesis is often reiterated by the atheologians. For example, Hume writes, "But might not other particular volitions remedy this inconvenience? In short, might not the Deity exterminate all ill, wherever it were to be found, and produce all good, without any preparation or long progress of causes and effects?"[10] And more recently William Rowe writes,

> Suppose in some distant forest lightning strikes a dead tree, resulting in a forest fire. In the fire a fawn is trapped, horribly burned, and lies in terrible agony for several days before death relieves its suffering. Could an omnipotent, omniscient being have prevented the fawn's apparently pointless suffering? The answer is obvious. An omnipotent, omniscient being could easily have prevented the fawn from being horribly burned, or, given the burning, could have spared the fawn the intense suffering by quickly ending its life. . . .[11]

For another thing, the atheologian argues, an omnipotent, omniscient, good, and loving deity could have instituted different laws in the first place, laws which would have resulted in less suffering than in fact takes place in this present world. For example, H. J. McCloskey writes,

> God could foresee man's emergence and could therefore have planned a world with better equipped sentient beings emerg-

ing. Of all the combinations of law-governed universes with emergent "men" that are possible for God, it seems very improbable . . . that an all-perfect being could not create a better world, and one with less evil in it, than this world. . . . God could modify or change the laws when evil could thereby be prevented or reduced.[12]

The upshot of the atheologian's argument is that there is good reason to expect less natural evil in the presence of a good and omnipotent deity than apart from his presence. Hence, following argument (1), one has good reason to believe that $P(E/N\&G) < P(E/N\&\overline{G})$. And if the prior probability $P(G/N)$ be put at ½, the result is that $P(G/N\&E) < $ ½, and depending on the degree to which one thinks this deity can intervene in particular cases, can alter the original natural laws, or could have created other natural laws, the disparity between $P(E/N\&G)$ and $P(E/N\&\overline{G})$ might be so great that the value of $P(G/N\&E)$ might be *much* less than ½. In this manner the atheologian can give some specificity to his inductive claim that the natural evil present in our world disconfirms God's existence. Similarly, following argument (2), the atheologian contends that one has prima facie reason to believe that since $P(E/N\&G) < P(E/N\&\overline{G})$, $P(G/N\&E) < P(G/N)$, showing that the natural evil present in our world tends to disconfirm God's existence.

THE THEIST'S RESPONSE

What response can the theist make to this inductive argument from evil? Four responses, I believe, are in order. *First*, in assigning the *prior probabilities* in argument (1), the atheologian has abstracted from and hence failed to consider the total evidence. But that G is improbable on N does not mean that G is improbable on N and T, where T is the total evidence minus N and E. For example, though

(M) Mary Carter has a college degree

is improbable on

(N) Mary Carter is an adult resident of Rochester, and 3 out
of 10 adult residents of Rochester have a college degree,

it is probable on (N) and

(O) Mary Carter is a business executive, and 95 out of 100
business executives in Rochester have a college degree.

With respect to the atheologian's inductive argument from evil, the theist might reasonably contend that the atheologian's exclusion of the theistic arguments or proofs for God's existence advanced by the natural theologian has skewed the results. The atheologian cannot exclude such evidence from N, for once included (as in N', where N' *includes* the theistic arguments) it would show that the prior probability $P(G/N')$ [or alternatively $P(G/N\&T)$] is much more than ½.

For the atheologian to reply that he does not recognize this alleged evidence or acknowledge the soundness or probability of the proofs does not suffice to answer this objection. Rather, what it raises is the larger question how one is to assign prior probabilities in disputed cases. Simply assigning probabilities of ½ in cases of dispute, where the two sides cannot agree on the significance of the evidence or purported evidence, is hardly an accurate procedure. If a mathematician and a young student were disputing whether 24 x 566 yielded 13,584 or 13,564, and if the student were stubbornly unconvinced by the mathematician's answer and argument, one would not then deign to assign the probability of ½ to both answers on the grounds that they could not agree on the matter. Mere disagreement is no basis for assigning such a (or any) probability. Neither can we assign probability on the basis of what the theist and atheologian both know. The fact that my knowledge includes information about optics and my son's does not has nothing to do with establishing the prior probability that light travels in waves rather than photons; it would be silly to assign a probability of ½ for everything which we do not know in common. On the other hand, neither can we make this probability simply relative to the noetic structure—the set of propositions a person believes, along with various logical and epistemic relations among these propositions—of either the theist or atheologian, for then the objectivity of the atheologian's inductive proof disappears, and the conclusion serves merely to inform us about the subjective beliefs of the various parties. In short, the inductive argument from natural evil considered in argument (1) fails in that it provides no way of establishing the prior probability of G on N in any objective manner or at the very least in any manner agreeable to both theist and atheologian. But unless one knows the prior probability of G on N, it is hard to see how any value can be assigned to $P(G/N\&E)$.

However, though this problem arises in a significant way for argument (1), it fails to affect argument (2), which in effect abstracts from assigning any particular value to the *prior probabilities*. In fact, the atheologian in argument (2) could incorporate the theistic arguments within N, *so long as* their probability was other than 0 or 1, for all he wants to show is that the natural evil occurring in the world *tends to disconfirm* God's existence. Thus argument (2) remains.

Secondly, the theist can question whether the evidence adduced by the atheologian supports the thesis that $P(E/N\&G) < P(E/N\&\overline{G})$. The atheologian has argued that good, powerful persons are capable of and frequently do intervene in the laws and states of affairs of nature so as to bring about less pain and suffering. Therefore it is reasonable to expect that

(P)   There will be less evil as the result of the activity of a good person than if he were not active,

and since God is a perfectly good person, we have

(Q)   There will be less evil as the result of God's activity than if he were not active.

But it would seem that what follows from the atheologian's evidence is not (P), for there are very many instances where the activity of good persons is not sufficient to alter the situation so as to prevent or reduce pain and suffering, for it would necessitate their performing an action they cannot perform. What does follow from the evidence is that it is reasonable to expect that

(R)   A good person would eliminate as much evil as he can without losing a greater good or bringing about an equal or greater evil.

Hence, it is reasonable to expect that

(S)   An omnipotent, omniscient, good, and loving personal God would eliminate as much evil as he can without losing a greater good or bringing about an equal or greater evil.

But from (S) it does not follow that $P(E/N\&G) < P(E/N\&\overline{G})$. This can be shown as follows. (S) is compatible with

(T)   God eliminates all the evil he can without losing a greater good or producing an equal or greater evil.

But (T) entails[13]

(U) $P(E/N\&G) \not< P(E/N\&\bar{G})$,

for since (T) affirms that God *eliminates* all evil for which there is no morally sufficient reason, the evil that does exist is the evil which is consonant with God's existence and nature, whereas if God did not exist, one would expect to find more evil, i.e., the evils which currently are eliminated by God. That is, one would expect, not E, but

> (E*) There are more than 10^6 turps of natural evil in the world.

Thus (S) is compatible with (U), and (U) is the contradictory of

(V) $P(E/N\&G) < P(E/N\&\bar{G})$.

Since (S) is compatible with (U) and (U) contradicts (V), (S) does not entail (V). Thus unless the atheologian can show that (Q) or (V) is true on other grounds, the conclusion of neither argument (1) nor (2) is established.

Thirdly, even granting (Q) will not establish the atheologian's case. Most theists hold that God is active in the world to prevent and eliminate evil. For Christians this is especially evident in God's redemptive activity, viewed both historically and eschatologically. The truth of (Q) does not entail that of (V), however, for by an argument similar to that just presented it can be shown that (Q) is compatible with (T) and hence with (U).

The atheologian, in reply, might argue that though (Q) does not entail (V), it does lend support to it, for if God did exist, one would expect there would be less evil than there is. That is, one would expect

> (F) There are less than 10^6 turps of natural evil in the world

to obtain. And if (V) is true, E disconfirms (given the proper prior probabilities) or tends to disconfirm God's existence.

The theist, on the other hand, could argue that what follows from (Q) is that if God did not exist, one would expect there would be more evil than there in fact is. That is, if God did not exist E* would obtain. Thus (Q) lends support to

(W) $P(E/N\&G) > P(E^*/N\&G)$.

Thus the existence of E does not disconfirm or tend to disconfirm God's existence, but with respect to E* is the lessened amount of evil one would expect from the activity of a good God.

In short, even granting (Q) we do not get an undisputed, decisive statement regarding what (Q) does or does not show. What this suggests is that the position one adopts in this regard vis-à-vis (U) or (V) depends on one's noetic structure, for it would seem that it is one's noetic structure which would account for the fact that from (Q) one draws (V) rather than (W) or vice versa.

Finally, is there any other way of determining whether $P(E/N\&G)$ is less than $P(E/N\&\overline{G})$? It might be thought that the atheologian could argue for this on the grounds that it is unreasonable to believe (T), i.e., that it is unreasonable to believe that God eliminates all the evil he can without losing a greater good or bringing about a greater evil.[15] This is not equivalent, however, to saying that it is reasonable to believe that God does *not* eliminate all the evil he can without losing a greater good or bringing about a greater evil. To say that it is unreasonable to believe p is not to affirm that it is reasonable to believe not-p. One might hold that it is reasonable to believe neither p nor not-p, given the evidence at hand: that is, it is more reasonable to be agnostic and withhold one's belief. Thus, the unreasonableness of (T), if it were so, would warrant only an agnostic response to whether God eliminates all the evil he can without losing a greater good or bringing about an equal or greater evil. As such the mere unreasonableness of belief in (T) fails to provide the atheologian with (V). What he must show is that it is reasonable to believe that (T) is false, and to do so he must show that it is reasonable to believe

> (X) There are instances of evil which, if God did exist, he could have eliminated without losing a greater good or producing an equal or greater evil

is true. But were we to grant (X) is true, does (V) follow from it? Clearly not, for (X) asserts that if God exists, there is evil compatible with his existence which he has not eliminated. On (X) alone we are not led to any expectations with respect to the amount of evil in the world, as (V) claims. Therefore another premiss, presumably (S), is needed in order to get (V).

What reason have we for thinking (X) to be true? To establish the truth of (X) or that we "have rational grounds for believing (X) to be true," atheologians often appeal to individual cases or classes of suffering which are apparently pointless.[16] Rowe, for example, cites the case of a fawn, trapped and burned in a forest fire, suffering for days before dying. This case and countless others like it, he contends, raise the question whether seemingly pointless suffering leads to some greater good. But individual cases or classes of cases of apparently pointless suffering do not help us decide the truth or falsity of (X), for they cannot provide the evidence needed to show that God *could* have prevented the suffering without losing a greater good. For one thing, the atheologian's argument seems to proceed along the illicit lines that since *we* could have prevented the suffering, *God* could have prevented the suffering [in the morally relevant sense of "could" specified in (X)]. For another, the atheologian's argument claims that instances of suffering which are seemingly or apparently pointless are in fact or likely pointless, for we do not know of any higher good to which they are a means. But this constitutes an appeal to ignorance; that we know of no higher good does not entail that there is no higher good or that one is unlikely. And even if the "unlikely" were granted, this argument would establish only the unreasonableness of believing (T), which as we have seen is insufficient to make the atheologian's case. Rowe comes at it a third way as well. He argues that even if the fawn's suffering is not really pointless, it is not reasonable to hold this to be the case in all instances of apparently pointless suffering.[17] But this begs the question; what needs to be shown is that there are such cases. Finally, even if the theist grants—as I think he should—that suffering in cases such as the unfortunate fawn is pointless or gratuitous, in that the particular fawn's suffering cannot be shown to be logically or causally necessary for there to be a greater good or for preventing a greater evil, this would not suffice to show that (X) is true. The principle involved in (X) is specified in (S). That principle asserts that God's existence and goodness, etc., are incompatible with his failure to eliminate or prevent as much evil as he can without losing some greater good or bringing about some greater evil. Suppose that there is some greater good. Then it follows that whatever is necessary for there being this greater good is such that its non-elimination, or better, its presence, is consistent with there being an omnipotent, good, etc., God. Clearly, this entails that *evils* which are logically or causally necessary for there to be this greater good are such that their presence in the actual world is consistent with God's existence, for to eliminate them or prevent them from obtaining would be to make impossible the greater good for which they are necessary. This also entails that *evils whose possibility* is logically necessary for there being this greater good are such that their presence is consistent with the existence of a good God, for if God would prevent these evils from being actual, he would be making their being-actual impossible, and to make their being-actual impossible is to make impossible this greater good for which their possibility was necessary. If we define pointless or gratuitous evils as evils which are not logically or causally necessary for there being a greater good, it follows that some instances of pointless or gratuitous evils, i.e., those whose possibility is necessary for there being a greater good or preventing a greater evil, are compatible with God's existence and goodness. For example, it might be argued that a world operating with regularity according to natural laws is a necessary condition for the greater good of the realization of moral values. But the former in turn necessitates the possibility of such natural evils as fawns suffering. The suffering of the fawn may be pointless or gratuitous, but the possibility of it is a necessary condition of there being that greater good.[18] Thus, the existence of pointless suffering whose possibility is necessary for there being a greater good or preventing a greater evil is compatible with the necessity that God eliminate as much evil as he can without losing a greater good or bringing about a greater evil, and hence with God's existence and goodness. Consequently, merely presenting instances of pointless suffering will not establish that there are instances of evil which God could have prevented, such that no overriding good would have been negatively affected by their prevention, i.e., that (X) is true or reasonably true. What the atheologian has to show is that this pointless suffering is not such that its possibility is necessary for there being the greater good—a tall order indeed.

Presenting individual cases of seemingly gratuitous evil,

therefore, will not suffice to make his case. What the atheologian must do to establish that (X) is reasonably true is show *both* that the theodicies and defenses proposed by the theist to show that there are no gratuitous evils other than those whose possibility is necessary for there being some greater good or preventing some greater evil are not sound *and* that there is good reason to expect that God would not have other good reasons for not eliminating more evil than he does. It will be remembered that it was theodicies and defenses which the atheologian had to exclude from N in order to make his prima facie case. The theist contends that once included in N, i.e., N*, there is no reason to think that the probability of E on N* and $\overline{G}$ is greater than on N* and G. If the atheologian *excludes* theodicies and defenses from N, his argument is inadequate in that in abstracting from the total evidence he has abstracted from important and perhaps decisive evidence. As argued above, that something is improbable on some evidence does not entail that it is improbable on the total evidence. If the atheologian *includes* evidence from theodicies and defenses, it would seem that there is no reason to think (X) true. The atheologian is therefore required at minimum to show that the proposed theodicies and defenses are unsound if he is to make his case for the truth of (X) and ultimately (V).

Even were he to succeed in refuting extant theodicies and defenses, however, there is less reason to think that he can show that there is good reason to expect that God would not have other good reasons for not eliminating more evil than he does, that the apparently pointless evil is really pointless and such that its possibility is not necessary for realizing the greater good. I do not know how the atheologian would propose to show this (though at the same time I do not think the theist can comfortably rest content solely with this defense). As we have seen, merely presenting individual cases of apparently pointless evils does not provide the relevant evidence, for such cases fail to show that what seems pointless is really pointless or that their mere pointlessness counts against (T).

In conclusion: it seems that the atheologian is no more successful with his evidential or inductive argument than with his deductive one. His inductive argument from evil does not disconfirm God's existence, nor has he presented relevant evidence to show that evil tends to disconfirm God's existence. Nor do the prospects appear bright that he can produce the relevant evidence. Thus it remains to be shown that the existence, variety, and profusion of evil make it irrational to believe in the existence of an omnipotent, omniscient, good, and loving personal God.

NOTES

1. William Rowe, *Philosophy of Religion* (Encino: Dickenson, 1978), pp. 80–86.

2. Rowe, p. 86.

3. David Hume, *Dialogues Concerning Natural Religion* (New York: Hafner, 1948), p. 73.

4. For the derivation of this theorem from the axioms of the elementary calculus of probability, see Wesley Salmon, *The Foundations of Scientific Inference* (Pittsburgh: University of Pittsburgh Press, 1966), pp. 58–63.

5. Wesley Salmon, "Religion and Science: A New Look at Hume's *Dialogues*," *Philosophical Studies* 33 (1978), 143–68.

6. Rowe, pp. 87f.; Hume, Parts X and XI.

7. Evil must be excluded from N, otherwise N would entail E, and the value of $P(E/N\&\bar{G})$ and $P(E/N\&G)$ would each be 1, with the result that $P(G/N\&E) = P(G/N)$. Morally sufficient reasons, defenses, and theodicies must be excluded in order to develop a prima facie case. The reasons for excluding construed evidence for God's existence will be spelled out and evaluated below.

8. H. J. McCloskey, *God and Evil* (The Hague: Nijhoff, 1974), pp. 8–10; Rowe, pp. 92–93.

9. For recent defenses of the cosmological argument see Bruce R. Reichenbach, *The Cosmological Argument: A Reassessment* (Springfield, Ill.: Thomas, 1972) and William L. Craig, *The Kalām Cosmo-*

logical Argument (London: Macmillan, 1979); for the ontological argument see Alvin Plantinga, *The Nature of Necessity* (London: Oxford University Press, 1974), Ch. 10, and Charles Hartshorne, *Anselm's Discovery* (LaSalle, Ill.: Open Court, 1965).

10. Hume, p. 74.

11. Rowe, p. 88.

12. McCloskey, pp. 94–95.

13. Of course, for his argument to succeed, the theist need not advocate the strong view that (T) entails (U); even the weaker contention that (T) is compatible with (U) will suffice to show that (S) is compatible with (U).

14. The idea of this counter-argument was suggested to me by Alvin Plantinga.

15. Rowe (p. 89) advocates this position: ". . . we must then ask whether it is reasonable to believe that *all* the instances of profound, seemingly pointless human and animal suffering lead to greater goods. And, if they should somehow all lead to greater goods, is it reasonable to believe that an omnipotent, omniscient being *could not* have brought about *any* of those goods without permitting the instances of suffering which supposedly lead to them? When we consider these more general questions in the light of our experience and knowledge of the variety and profusion of human and animal suffering occurring daily in our world, it seems that the answer must be *no*."

16. Rowe stresses that it is not that we know with certainty or can prove that these cases do not lead to some greater good, but that it is unlikely they do, such that we "have *rational grounds* for believing [(X)] to be true" (p. 88).

17. Rowe, p. 89.

18. We will develop this view in Chapter 5.

3

Presuppositions

PRESUPPOSITIONS ARE BOTH A BOON AND A BANE to the philosopher. As a boon, they provide the philosopher with his philosophical fare. Indeed, what would the philosopher do were it not for presuppositions to be ferreted out of other philosophers' arguments! As a bane, they are the source of endless trouble. If left implicit, like a beast they are ruthlessly hunted, tracked to their lair, flushed from their hiding place, and exposed for all to see. If stated explicitly, they are open to critical attack, and being what they are, they often stand bare and defenseless before the onslaught. As non-deducible, they rest on less sure legs of justification, their stability more or less strong depending on the eye of the beholder. Yet presuppositions frequently must be made, and dealing with the problem of evil presents no exception. The atheologian's presuppositions (9) and (X) came under scrutiny in Chapters 1 and 2. Here we must state and defend our own, i.e, the presuppositions a theist might deem true in order to construct an adequate theodicy for evil.

In this chapter I will present four definitions and four presuppositions. The presuppositions I take to express necessary truths. Were they merely contingently true, then there could be other possible worlds in which they were not true. But the crux of our argument will be that for beings of a certain sort (moral agents) to exist in any world, certain states of affairs are required. Thus, these propositions must be true in all possible worlds.

DEFINITIONS

Let us begin with definitions of some terms which will be used in the subsequent argument.

> D$_1$ A being x is omnipotent if and only if it is capable of bringing about any contingent state of affairs (a) whose description does not contain or entail a contradiction, and (b) whose description does not exclude or entail the exclusion of x or any omnipotent agent from among those which may have brought about that state of affairs.[1]

As we argued in Chapter 1, this definition of omnipotence, rather than that which defines it as being able to do anything whatsoever, is necessary both to the solution and to the problem of evil. Unless it is impossible for God to do that whose description contains or entails a contradiction, the problem of evil is no problem at all, for the lack of a morally sufficient reason for evil, though incompatible with God's goodness, would not mean that God did not exist or lacked certain essential properties. If he could perform that whose description contains or entails a contradiction, he then could do evil and still be perfectly good.

We shall have more to say about this definition in Chapter 8. There we shall argue that this definition is not narrow enough in that it allows some possible beings which possess all their limited number of properties essentially to be omnipotent. We shall also raise the question whether it is true that God is omnipotent, and whether a God finite in power might not also be the reason there is so much evil present in the world. In the intervening four chapters, however, we shall assume that God is omnipotent and shall utilize this definition as adequate for our purposes.

> D$_2$ An action is morally significant for a given person at a given time if and only if it would be wrong for him to

perform the action then but right to refrain, or vice versa.[2]

Morally significant actions contrast with other actions which are such that either doing them or not doing them is morally neutral. For example, whether I take Dale Street or Lexington Avenue to the expressway, or whether I write this sentence using a pen or a pencil is, generally speaking, not a morally significant choice, for one would neither praise nor blame me for taking or using one rather than the other.

> D_3 A person is significantly free, on a given occasion, if he is then free either to perform or to refrain from performing an action that is morally significant for him.[3]

Finally,

> D_4 A miracle is a special act of God whereby for a moral or spiritual purpose he produces in nature a new being or mode of being.

There are four aspects to this definition. First, as a special act, it describes a state of affairs in which an additional causal element—the activity of God—has been specifically introduced, such that what results is not what would result were the additional causal element absent. This then accounts for the unusual or extraordinary element perceived by us, for whereas the individual expected that, given cause ABC, D would occur, E occurred. The observer is surprised; the event is a cause of wonder. But what the observer did not know or had not taken into account was the fact that the cause was $ABCG_{od}$, in which case, since an additional causal condition was added, a different effect should be expected.

Secondly, a miracle is an act of God. Since this precludes other agents, one might inquire whether people like Elijah

(1 Kgs. 17:17–24, 18:17–39), Peter (Acts 3:1–9), Paul (Acts 20:9–12), or the saints have performed miracles. This seems particularly important in some traditions in that the performance of miracles is deemed a necessary condition for being a saint. One reply to this might be that though the saint did not produce the miracle, the saint (or another individual) was the occasion for the miracle, for God's special act is his response to the prayers and requests of the saint.

Thirdly, as occurring for a moral or spiritual purpose, a miracle is a conscious act of God wherein he acts purposively to further his ends. Thus, as C. S. Lewis suggests,[4] there is a fittingness about true miracles. They are not haphazard or random, but can be seen to fit into a divine program—as, for example, centering on the redemption of man. Neither is it the case that any extraordinary event is truly a miracle. That the tornado hopped over the trailer court without doing any damage, that the train carrying dangerous chemicals derailed and exploded in an unpopulated area, that Robert's soup spilled on his bib rather than on his overalls, that I woke up at the right time even though I forgot to set the alarm clock, might be examples of unusual and fortunate events, but not necessarily miracles. "To be a miracle an event must contribute significantly towards a holy divine purpose for the world."[5]

Fourthly, a miracle can result either in the production of a totally new creation (as in the re-creation of the individual person at the end time) or in some present existent's being modified (as, e.g., the water changed by Jesus into wine at Cana [Jn. 2:1–10] or the burning bush encountered by Moses [Ex. 3:1–4]).

Our concern in what follows will be not with establishing whether miracles are possible or actually occur, or indeed with individual miracles at all, but rather with whether the world can be run or operated by divine miraculous intervention. For our purposes we shall assume that miracles are possible; were miracles logically impossible, our case would be made substantially easier, for then our point could be established strictly by logical inference from this impossibility.

PRESUPPOSITIONS

The theist's case also requires four presuppositions, which for reasons stated above must be understood as necessary truths.

> P_1 A world containing significantly free persons making choices between moral good and evil and choosing a significant amount of moral good is superior to a world lacking significantly free persons and moral good and evil.

Perhaps one way of seeing the truth of this proposition is to look at our own decision-making. In choosing to procreate children rather than to have robots made for us, we are consciously or subconsciously affirming P_1, for though by having robots made we could be certain of the outcome of their existence—what they could do for us and what actions they would and would not perform—yet we desire the response of free persons, even though we do not know that in the end they will love and respond to us, what values they will adopt, or what moral choices they will make. We assume from our experience that with proper training it will be the case that they will choose a significant amount of moral good and will experience a significant amount of happiness and satisfaction.

The evaluation of superiority in P_1 includes not only the moral good chosen or achieved, but also the existence of persons making these choices and realizing the moral good. It might be argued that the existence of persons who are moral agents is itself intrinsically valuable. If this is so, it need not be the case that more moral good than evil is chosen; only that the significant amount of moral good actualized and the good resulting from there being significantly free persons exceed the moral evil actualized and the evil which would result from the non-existence of significantly free persons.

Now, just as there can be no moral good in the world without there being moral agents to actualize it, so neither can there be moral agents unless there are beings who are significantly free. Thus our second presupposition:

P₂ For a person to be a moral agent, he must be at times significantly free.

To be a moral agent, an individual must be capable of performing morally significant actions, and according to D₂ an action is morally significant for a person when to perform the action is right and not to perform the action is wrong, or vice versa. This entails, from the objective side, that more than one option be open to the person. In particular, there must be the option of performing the action and the option of not performing the action. From the subjective side, it must be possible for the person either to perform the action or to refrain from performing it. Put in the past tense, if the person performed action x he could just as well have not performed x, or vice versa. If by "being free" we mean "could have done otherwise," then with respect to these options the person must be free, and it cannot be the case that he is compelled to do either one or the other. Were he compelled or determined, the action would not be morally significant for *him* at that time. And were all actions determined or compulsory, there would be no morally significant actions for that person, and thus he would not be a moral agent.

Perhaps we can put this another way. A moral agent is one to whom moral oughts apply. That is, he ought to do the right and he ought to avoid the wrong. But that P ought to do x entails that there is open to P another option besides doing x; P also must be able not to do x. Where there is only one course of action possible, where it is impossible for P to choose or act in another way, the ought loses its significance. There is then no ought, only an is. Further, if the ought is to have any significance for P, it must be possible for P either to do x or to refrain from doing x. It makes no sense to say that P ought to do x when P is compelled to do x or when P is compelled to refrain from doing x. There is, then, a connection between "ought" and "can." To say that P has a moral obligation to do x rather than to refrain from doing x entails that P can either do x or not do x: both doing x and not doing x are possible for P in that circumstance. And as such, P is free. Thus, if oughts are to apply to P, P must be capable of either doing x (where doing x is right) or refraining from doing x: that is, he must be significantly free.

Our third presupposition

P₃ No person can be held morally accountable for that which he could not have done otherwise

follows from P₂ with the aid of two premisses. The first,

A₁ All persons who can be held morally accountable for their actions are moral agents,

seems unobjectionable. The second

A₂ All persons who are significantly free are persons who could have done otherwise (than they did)

follows from what it means to be free. As noted above, by "being free" is meant "could have done otherwise."

Thus, using D_3, a person who is significantly free, on a given occasion, can either perform or refrain from performing an action that is morally significant for him. Or to put it in the past tense, a person who is significantly free, given certain conditions, could have chosen or done otherwise than he did. As significantly free, alternative courses of moral action must be genuine possibilities.

A fourth presupposition might be added to enable us to apply a general theodicy to the present world.

> P_4 Human persons are beings capable of morally significant actions.

As a necessary truth, P_4 asserts that human persons are essentially moral agents, capable of making moral choices and performing moral actions.

In what follows we shall employ these presuppositions in our endeavor to provide a morally sufficient reason for both moral and natural evil.

LIBERTARIANISM

From what has been said above and in Chapter 1 it should be apparent that our discussion presumes a categorical interpretation of "could have done otherwise." According to the view we will be espousing in this book, an agent is free if, given the same conditions, he could have chosen or done otherwise than he did. Though certain causal conditions are present and indeed may be necessary for an agent to choose or act in a certain way, if he is free, these causal conditions are not sufficient to cause or determine him to choose or act in that fashion. The individual himself is the sufficient condition for the course of action chosen, but there are no causal conditions sufficient to cause him to choose that course of action.

Thus, human freedom is incompatible with causal determinism. If the individual human person is externally compelled (by force of any type which is irresistible) or internally determined (by his genetic constitution or the action of a deity), then he is not free. If his choice or action follows necessarily from the external or internal determinants, it is not truly his choice, for he lacks the ability to select between the influences and the alternative courses of action. Of course, this should not be taken to mean that freedom is the absence of influences, including external and internal causal conditions. Rather, it means that these conditions are not determinative of the agent's choice or action. On this view of freedom, then, knowledge of all prior conditions in the universe and all natural laws will not enable someone to predict *with certainty* that the agent will choose x rather than y, or choose x rather than refrain from choosing x.

This is not to say that the choice made is arbitrary or that the act is an instance of chance or random indeterminacy. There are reasons which can be given relevant to the action chosen, reasons of varying soundness and appeal, but reasons nonetheless. These reasons might include the ends desired, the dispositions, likes and dislikes of the agent, and the environmental factors or conditions present. On the one hand, these reasons can and probably do include necessary causal conditions for the choice made or action performed, but the causal conditions are not determinative of the choice or action. On the other hand, there are likewise non-causal reasons present, reasons which the agent, as free, has the power to consider, evaluate, weigh, and appraise. He can accept reasons which are sound and rationally compelling or he can reject the most telling or valid reasons and choose according to others. But whichever is the case, the action or choice is explicable and not arbitrary.

It is true that, as so analyzed, the free choices or actions are not a product of prior conditions which are necessary and sufficient to produce that choice or action. However, there is no reason to restrict explanation to explanation of this type. Explanations can also be given in terms of reasons, where reasons include the aims, goals, purposes, or ends desired, as well as the necessary causal conditions. Thus, for example, one might explain my going to the store in terms of my wanting to get milk and eggs for tomorrow's breakfast. That no complete causal account can be given for my free act of going to the store does not make that act any less intelligible. Neither does the fact that purposes and aims cannot be reduced to causal conditions make the former any less of an explanation. My action is not random or arbitrary, but explicable in terms of the relevant purposes and the requisite causal conditions.

Neither should this view be understood as equating freedom with unpredictability. That the agent can choose contrary to past choices or his character—compare "He acted out of character at the party"—does not entail that he will so choose, or even that it is likely that he will so choose. Generally it would seem reasonable to expect that the agent will choose in a pattern consistent with previous choices, that the reasons the agent accepted in the past he will continue to accept and use in the future. If this is true, then P can predict with some accuracy what Q will choose to do by (1) noting what Q did on past occasions which had circumstances similar to this one, and (2) learning the reasons Q gives for taking the courses of action he does, and then observing in what circumstances and how consistently these reasons are used. The charge of unpredictability is based on a confusion; one should not confuse possibility (that the agent can do otherwise than he normally does) with probability (that it is likely that the agent will do otherwise than he normally does and hence is unpredictable).

This view, often called the Incompatibilist or Libertarian view, must be distinguished from the Compatibilist view. The Compatibilist likewise contends that an individual is free when he could have done otherwise than he did. But he understands "could have done otherwise" in a hypothetical sense. By "could have done otherwise" he means that if certain other conditions had been fulfilled or present, an effect different from what did occur would have occurred. For example, if the agent had chosen differently or really tried or if there had been no external compulsion to act in a certain way, he would have done otherwise. As such, the Compatibilist rejects the categorical interpretation of "could have done otherwise."

By using the hypothetical sense of "could have done otherwise" freedom is viewed as compatible with determinism. For the Compatibilist the determination of whether an individual acts freely is not dependent upon the presence or absence of antecedent (or better, non-subsequent) causal conditions. Though a precise analysis of all the non-subsequent conditions would enable someone (in principle) to know what the individual would choose or do, the individual still is free when he could have done otherwise than he did if certain other conditions had been in effect, for "being able to do otherwise if . . ." in no way precludes that the agent's action is the necessary result of certain non-subsequent causal conditions. "There is no contradiction involved in saying that a particular action or choice was *both* free, and could have been helped, and so on; *and* predictable, or even foreknown, and explicable in terms of caused causes."[6] Rather, the determination of whether an individual acts freely depends upon whether the individual was able to act according to what he willed. If the individual is prevented from acting as he wills, he cannot do otherwise and hence is not free.

In moral contexts statements about what some person

could or could not have done are not about whether one's behavior is the product of heredity or environment, but about the ascription of moral responsibility. And we can ascribe moral responsibility where a person is free, i.e., is able to do what he wills. Whether or not there were non-subsequent causal conditions sufficient to bring about the action is irrelevant to the freedom of the agent vis-à-vis his action. What is required is that the person knew what he was doing, was not compelled to do it against his will (no persons or external circumstances prevented him from doing what he wanted to do or compelled him to do what he did not want to do), and that he can be influenced so that he will change his behavior. "Threats and promises, punishments and rewards, the ascription of responsibility and the nonascription of responsibility, have therefore a clear pragmatic justification which is quite consistent with a wholehearted belief in metaphysical determinism."[7] Smart gives the example of the lazy versus the slow student. The lazy and apathetic student is morally responsible for his poor performance, and the instructor can hold him morally accountable and subject to punishment because he can do better. He could apply himself conscientiously to his next assignment, do the appropriate research, and turn in a paper of high quality. Accordingly, the instructor will punish or correct him, and consequently introduce additional causal factors in order to bring about this desired change in the student's behavior. On the other hand, a slow student cannot be held morally accountable for his poor work, for no amount of chiding or punishment will banish his slowness. Even if he willed it, he could not perform better. Thus, only of the first student is it meaningful to say that he was free and could have done otherwise than he did and that he can be held morally accountable for his poor academic performance. A person, then, is morally responsible only if he is modifiable by praise or blame, if punishment or reward will or would have affected his choice.

But suppose we take the case of the so-called hardened criminal. That is, suppose there is a person P who knows the difference between right and wrong and who enjoys committing crimes; performing criminal acts has such a strong appeal to him that no matter how P is punished (or rewarded) he always returns to a life of crime. On the compatibilist thesis, since P's behavior is not modifiable by punishment (or reward), he cannot do otherwise and hence is not to be held morally accountable for his acts. Neither would it be appropriate to punish him, since his behavior is not modifiable. But both of these consequences seem wrong. It certainly is true that P could do otherwise; he enjoys and freely chooses the life of crime and could at any time not do the criminal act. That he is consistent in his choices does not mean that he is not free. Further, it would be most appropriate to punish him, despite his unmodifiability. Justice would seem to require that he be punished for his freely chosen acts.

The Libertarian will agree with the conclusion regarding moral responsibility to which Smart comes in his example of the students. He will agree that the lazy student is morally accountable and the slow one not. But he will agree with the conclusion based upon different reasons. The case of the hardened criminal reveals the implausibility of the reasoning which the Compatibilist uses to derive or support his conclusion.

The issue between the Compatibilist and the Incompatibilist centers on what is meant by "could have done otherwise." It seems odd indeed to speak of freedom, as the Compatibilist does, as the ability to have done otherwise *if* certain conditions had been different. Free choice with respect to a particular event appears to refer to the possibility of there having occurred a different outcome, given the same physical state of affairs, not to the possibility of there having obtained a different set of initial conditions. Freedom operates within a certain set of given conditions; it is not a relation between different sets of conditions and their effects.

Lest we conclude too hastily, it might be helpful to reconstruct the argument which the Compatibilist gives in support of his contention. The Compatibilist Antony Flew argues that we can have both "true action" and "genuine choice" without the necessity of libertarian free will's being involved. To support this, Flew introduces two cases, one where a bank manager, threatened by a robber with a gun, removes money from the bank safe, and the other where a person is thrown through a shop window by a gang of thugs. In the first case, he says, we would want to say that the manager engaged in true action, whereas in the second case the person did not engage in true action, but rather was a passive victim of the action of the thugs. Furthermore, in the first case the manager had a genuine choice: he could either remove the money from the safe or resist the robber, though of course in peril of his life. In the second case, however, the human missile did not have a choice: he was tossed through the window by others. Thus, in the first case the manager engaged in true action and had a genuine choice, whereas in the second neither was the case.

Neither person is free (unconstrained), Flew continues, nor is each morally accountable, though for different reasons. The manager could not be held morally accountable for the missing money because he was compelled to remove the money. On the other hand, the human missile cannot be held morally accountable, not because he was compelled to act, but because he did not act as an agent at all.

From this it follows, Flew argues, that the manager can both be compelled to act and be an agent who engages in true action and genuine choice. But since "whenever it is correct to say that someone acts or chooses it must surely be equally correct to say that, in some fundamental sense, he could have acted or chosen otherwise,"[8] the manager was both compelled to do a specific act and could have done or chosen otherwise. That is, it is possible for a person to be under compulsion to perform a particular act and still be able to do otherwise. From this he concludes to the compatibilist thesis that genuine choice does not entail free will.

We might attempt to formalize Flew's argument as follows:

(1) It is not the case that one can both have free will and be determined. [By definition of Libertarian free will.]

(2) It is possible for a person to be compelled to do x and to have genuine choice with respect to x.

(3) If one is compelled to do x, that he does x is determined (i.e., has "contingently sufficient non-subsequent conditions").

(4) ∴ It is possible for a person to be determined to do x and still have genuine choice with respect to x. [2 & 3]

(5) ∴ If a person is determined to do x, he does not have free will. [1]

(6) ∴ It is possible for a person to have genuine choice with respect to x and not have free will. [4 & 5]

(7) ∴ It is not the case that "that a person has genuine choice with respect to x" entails that he has free will. [6]

The conclusions follow validly; granting (1), the premisses that need closer scrutiny are (2) and (3). How does Flew propose to defend them?

Flew defends (2) by appealing to the example of the bank manager who encounters the robber brandishing the pistol. It is certainly true that the manager had a choice with regard to the money in the vault—he could either remove it or refuse to remove it. Either would have constituted, using Flew's language, a true action. But is this a case of compulsion? Flew argues that it is, on the grounds that the manager, if charged with immoral conduct, could exculpate himself by arguing that the presence of the pistol and the verbal threat accompanying it compelled him to take the money, and "this plea in this case is, very properly, accepted as a complete excuse."[9]

Now, if this be a case of compulsion, it surely is a different sense of compulsion from that found in the case of the human missile. This Flew admits. The latter, he argues, is a case of compulsion upon a victim; it would seem roughly equivalent to what Aristotle termed "violence." The former is compulsion upon an agent. In referring to this type of case Flew uses such synonyms as "constrained" and "acting under pressure." For him "being compelled to do x" is the contradictory of the "ordinary" (non-metaphysical) meaning of free, where free is taken to mean that a person "did what he did and rejected possible alternative courses of action without being under pressure to act in this way."[10] To be free is to have no obstruction to carrying out one's action if one chooses otherwise. It is not the presence or absence of alternative courses of action per se which is critical here, for Flew writes that "there always is some alternative in cases of acting under compulsion, . . . the agent always does in some more fundamental sense have a choice."[11] Rather, what seems critical to Flew's understanding of acting under compulsion is being under pressure to choose one alternative rather than another, pressure which, depending on "the severity of the threat and the seriousness of the offence,"[12] can be sufficient to remove moral accountability for the action. In the case of the bank manager, he acted under constraint or pressure which was so severe in light of the offense committed (supposing he took the money) that it removed moral accountability.[13]

If we understand "being compelled to do x" as acting

under severe pressure to reject possible alternative courses of action, then we can grant the truth of (2). That is, it is possible for an agent to act under compulsion or constraint and still have genuine choice (be able to do other than he did). But what about (3)? Is it the case, as (3) claims, that compulsion thus understood is an instance of determinism? Is the compulsion which the manager pleads in his behalf—the presence of the threat and the gun—the compulsion of determinism? That there were causal factors in his decision cannot be denied, but to say this is not to establish causal determinacy. What is absent from Flew's argument is any reason to think that the presence of the gun causally determined the manager to choose one way rather than another, and thus he has provided no evidence that (3) is true. Indeed, it is possible that the presence of the threat and gun was not determinative, for the Libertarian could contend that no one, knowing all the precedent conditions, could deduce with certainty what the manager would do (recall the joke about the mugger who approached Jack Benny and demanded "Your money or your life." After a long pause and repetition of the demand by the robber, Benny replied, "I'm thinking! I'm thinking!"), though certainly he could provide a reasonable prediction by knowing something about the bank manager or about human agents' choices in general. But *certain* prediction should be possible if compulsion here is an instance of determinism.

Of course, Flew cannot use the example of the human missile as evidence in favor of (3), for then he would be guilty of equivocation, for the compulsion in the case of the manager and in the case of the human missile differ. The latter is an instance of "violence" and is truly determinative; but were this the type of compulsion present in the case of the bank manager—e.g., were his hand moved by the robber to remove the money—then, though here we would have an instance in which the compulsion is determinative, we would no longer have an example showing (2) to be true, for, as Flew notes, the manager would be no longer an agent but a victim.

In short, if "being compelled to do x" be understood as "acting under severe pressure to reject possible alternative courses of action," then though the case of the manager establishes the truth of (2), Flew provides no reason to think that (3) is true—i.e., that where there is compulsion there is a set of causally sufficient, nonsubsequent conditions for the agent's action. On the other hand, if "being compelled to do x" be understood to refer to the kind of victim compulsion present in the case of the human missile, then though the truth of (3) can be granted, there is no reason to think (2) is true, for to have a genuine choice there must be an agent, not a victim. Therefore, Flew's argument to establish the compatibilist thesis fails.[14]

Of course, the failure of Flew's argument does not establish Libertarianism. However, in what follows we shall assume the Libertarian view of human freedom. In particular, we shall take as contradictory the claim that one agent can bring it about, either directly or indirectly by constituting the nature of the agent in a determinate manner, that another agent freely chooses or acts in a certain way. We shall hold that to be caused to do action x is incompatible with doing x freely.

NOTES

1. Adapted from George Mavrodes, "Defining Omnipotence," *Philosophical Studies* 32 (1977), 199–200. For a critique of Mavrodes' definition, see my "Mavrodes on Omnipotence," *Philosophical Studies* 37 (1980), 211–14.

2. Alvin Plantinga, *The Nature of Necessity* (London: Oxford University Press, 1974), p. 166.

3. Adapted from Plantinga, p. 166.

4. C. S. Lewis, *Miracles* (New York: Macmillan, 1947), p. 110.

5. Richard Swinburne, *The Concept of Miracle* (New York: St. Martin's Press, 1970), p. 8.

6. Antony Flew, "Divine Omnipotence and Human Freedom," in Antony Flew and Alasdair MacIntyre, edd., *New Essays in Philosophical Theology* (New York: Macmillan, 1955), p. 151.

7. J. J. C. Smart, "Free Will, Praise and Blame," *Mind* 70, No. 279 (July 1961), reprinted in Gerald Dworkin, ed., *Determinism, Free Will and Moral Responsibility* (Englewood Cliffs, N.J.: Prentice-Hall, 1970), p. 209.

8. Antony Flew, "Compatibilism, Free Will and God," *Philosophy* 48 (1973), 234.

9. Flew, "Compatibilism, Free Will and God," 234.

10. Flew, "Divine Omnipotence and Human Freedom," 149–50.

11. Flew, "Compatibilism, Free Will and God," 235.

12. Flew, "Compatibilism, Free Will and God," 235.

13. This is Flew's way of putting it. I would want to argue that what the presence of the threat and the gun did was to remove the *genuine* choice of the manager. The manager had a choice between two options, but he lacked genuine choice. (Flew also uses the term "genuine choice," which he does not define; however, his usage of "choice" and "genuine choice" seems to make "genuine" of no added significance.) Genuine choice occurs when the options the individual is faced with are ones which the individual could reasonably be expected to choose. That is, there must be a reasonableness about both options. This involves, among other things, the possibility of a qualitative and quantitative measurability between them. In the case of the bank manager he has another option besides obeying the robber's command; he could refuse to take the money. But it is not a reasonable alternative, for there exists no measurability between the options. The manager's life is not qualitatively on a par with a limited amount of money. If the circumstances were altered, however, such that the robber orders him not to steal but to slay two other individuals, the choice between his death and the death of the others might indeed constitute a genuine option, for there now exists a measure of qualitative and quantitative comparison between his life and the lives of the others.

14. Flew suggests another argument for Compatibilism which is ad hominem against the theistic Libertarian. He contends that the Libertarian doctrine of human freedom is incompatible with certain basic theistic tenets, in particular the doctrines of creation and divine providence.

Flew argues that according to the theistic doctrine of providence, "God is the ultimate sufficient condition not only of all motion but also of all movings" ("Compatibilism, Free Will and God," 240). He quotes Aquinas to the effect that "just as God not only gave being to things when they first began, but is also—as the conserving cause of being—the cause of their being as long as they last . . . ; so he also not only gave things their operative powers when they were first created, but is also always the cause of these in things. Hence, if this divine influence stopped every operation would stop. Every operation, therefore, of anything is traced back to him as its cause. . . . God alone can move the will, as an agent, without doing violence to it. . . . Hence we receive from God not only the power of willing but its employment also" (Flew, 240; *Summa contra Gentiles*, III, 67, 88–89).

This is not the place to attempt to disentangle the variety of difficulties found in the doctrine of divine providence. But two things at least must be said. First, though Aquinas may not be fully consistent, yet his repeated claim is that providence as applied to humans neither excludes freedom of choice nor implies a necessity upon the agent's action (*Summa contra Gentiles* 73n1, 88n5, 90n9, 94n12, 163n2). In the passages quoted by Flew it appears that Aquinas has in mind the view that God is a *necessary* causal condition for every agent's action. God is the necessary condition for every act in that not only does he preserve all agents in being, but he enables all agents to operate by supplying the power by which the agent acts (66n1, 67n1, 70n5). It is true, however, that Aquinas at times also seems to suggest that God is the *sufficient* condition for human acts. He writes, "So, in the function of providential foresight, by means of the sempiternal meditative act of His wisdom, He orders all things, no matter how detailed they may appear; and whatever things perform any action, they instrumentally, as moved by Him" (94n10). In man God inclines the will as an agent to a particular end (88n4). Yet Aquinas affirms that the effects can be intended by God to be established contingently; even the inclination of the individual's will occurs non-causally from within (in that God as that which all desire moves the individual to will a certain good which is his end), and hence he is not determined or in violence moved so as to violate the freedom of the will. Whether it is consistent to hold that "the divine motion is infallible and efficacious in regard to every detail of the creature's decision, . . . yet [insofar as] it takes place entirely on the plane of freedom it exercises no violence, no coercion, no compulsion" (Joseph Owens, *An Elementary Christian Metaphysic* [Milwaukee: Bruce, 1963], p. 362) is doubtful; Thomistic writers contend that we cannot form a "proper concept" of it, that we know both statements are true but how they fit together remains a "mystery" to a finite mind limited to knowing God by analogy. Yet it does register Aquinas' attempt to hold to both divine providence and a Libertarian view of human freedom.

Secondly, and apart from the specific arguments in Aquinas, divine providence can be understood to encompass three things. First, it includes God's act of causing and sustaining all creatures in existence. That is,

God (as a necessary being) is the necessary condition for the existence of every contingent being. Without him nothing would exist. Providence so understood involves not merely his creative and sustaining activity, but his ordering of creation to divinely appointed ends as well. Secondly, it includes his provision of good for all his creatures. The doctrine of providence affirms that God cares for his creation, seeking the best for it and directing it toward the fulfillment of the ends for which the world was created. Though his provision can be at times miraculous, it is generally ordered through the secondary causes of nature. This provision through nature in no way entails any disregard of human freedom; rather, God can be seen as caring for his creation and accomplishing his purposes by cooperating with and responding to our own wills. Thirdly, providence includes God's salvific plans for man and Nature, wherein God acts in history to reconcile man to himself and ultimately to create Nature anew. Again, providence may be seen working in and through man's freely chosen acts, as well as in response to them. In all of this no conflict between Libertarianism and divine providence need be envisioned.

4

Theodicy for Moral Evils

As DEFINED IN THE PREFACE, moral evils are those evils which result from acts for which human agents can be held morally accountable. In performing such actions, these agents are moral agents. But according to P_2, for a person to be a moral agent, he must be at times significantly free. That is, to be a moral agent he must be free with respect to actions which are morally significant for him, such that doing a certain action at a certain time is morally right and refraining from doing it then is morally wrong, or vice versa. According to P_1 a world containing significantly free persons making moral choices between moral good and evil and choosing a significant amount of moral good is superior to a world lacking significantly free persons and moral good and evil. Thus, it was consistent with God's goodness that he create a world inhabited by significantly free persons.

But in a world inhabited by significantly free persons whether there is moral evil or not depends upon these free persons. It is up to them whether they will choose to do right or wrong in a morally significant situation. If they are capable of doing right, at the same time they are capable of doing wrong. If they choose to do wrong, God cannot prevent them from doing that wrong, or even choosing it, without removing their significant freedom, and should he consistently do this so as to remove all moral evil, he would then be bringing about an inferior world [P_1]. Thus, since to bring about the higher good it was necessary that moral evil be possible, God cannot be held morally ac-

countable or blameworthy for the moral evil that free
agents choose or perform [P₃].

Several objections have been raised against this theodicy.
The most serious objection is one raised by J. L. Mackie
and repeated by others. Mackie writes,

> . . . [I]f God has made men such that in their free choices
> they sometimes prefer what is good and sometimes what is
> evil, why could he not have made men such that they always
> freely choose the good? If there is no logical impossibility
> in a man's freely choosing the good once, or on several oc-
> casions, there cannot be a logical impossibility in his freely
> choosing the good on every occasion. God was not, then,
> faced with a choice between making innocent automata and
> making beings who, in acting freely, would sometimes go
> wrong: there was open to him the obviously better possi-
> bility of making beings who would act freely but always go
> right. Clearly, his failure to avail himself of this possibility
> is inconsistent with his being both omnipotent and wholly
> good.[1]

More recently H. J. McCloskey reiterates the same objection, writing that God could "cause only those who will be
morally good to come into being."[2]

The argument given here, which we considered in Chapter 1, is as follows [utilizing the notation of Chapter 1 for
the first three premisses]:

(10) That the only free agents which come into being are
those which, when they choose between doing good
and doing evil, always choose the good, is a state of
affairs the description of which does not contain or
entail a contradiction.

(11) God as omnipotent can bring about all states of af-

fairs the description of which does not contain or entail a contradiction.

(12) ∴ God as omnipotent can bring it about that the only free agents which come into being are those which, when they choose between doing good and doing evil, always choose the good.

(17) If all free agents which come into being, when they choose between doing good and doing evil, always choose the good, there will be no moral evil.

(18) ∴ God as omnipotent can bring it about that there will be no moral evil.

Accordingly, the presence of moral evil suggests either that God is not good, all-powerful, or that he does not exist.

Our response in Chapter 1 to this argument can be re-iterated. One must be careful to note precisely what is asserted in (12). If (12) be taken to assert that

(14) God as omnipotent can bring it about that all free agents, when they choose between doing good and doing evil, always choose the good,

then since it is God who brings it about that they choose the good, their choices are determined by God. Thus they cannot be called free agents. A being cannot be said to be caused by another to choose freely. As such (14) contains a contradiction and does not describe a state of affairs one would expect God to be able to bring about. If, on the other hand, (12) be taken to assert that

(15) God as omnipotent can bring about the existence of free agents which, when they choose between doing good and doing evil, always choose the good,

then there is no contradiction. God, according to (15), can bring about the existence of certain free persons, and it is logically possible that they always choose the good. Of course, it is also logically possible that they choose both good and evil, or even that they choose always to do evil. What the individuals that God creates choose is up to them as significantly free moral agents; God cannot bring it about that these created persons will always choose the good freely, which was asserted in (14). But if (12) be understood as (15), it does not follow that God can bring it about that there will be no moral evil: whether or not there is moral evil depends on the choices which the individuals created by God make. If they do choose to do the good, then there will be no moral evil; but God cannot bring this about without violating their free agency.

We might put this objection another way, utilizing a distinction made by Plantinga between strong and weak actualization. He writes, "We must make a corresponding distinction, then, between a stronger and a weaker sense of 'actualize.' In the strong sense, God can actualize only what he can *cause* to be actual";[3] i.e., he strongly actualizes a given state of affairs S only if he causes it to be the case that S is actual. In the weak sense of actualize, God brings it about that something S happens if and only if there is another state of affairs which God has brought about, and God knows that if such a state of affairs is actual, then S will happen (be actual). In this sense God does not directly bring about all states of affairs; however, it is the case that he is responsible for causing or creating a certain being (person B) who then freely brings about a certain state of affairs S (eating a peanut butter sandwich for lunch.) Thus it can be said that God permits or allows that state of affairs S to become actual insofar as he is the sufficient condition for the existence of the being who chooses to perform that action, knows what that being will do, and continues that person's existence.

We might now reformulate Mackie's thesis as a question: Could God actualize a state of affairs which only included the existence of creatures who freely always do the

right? In the strong sense of actualize, it is the case that
God himself brings about a certain state of affairs. If it is
the case that God himself brings about the state of affairs
which includes these moral agents' choosing or performing the good, then their choice or action was determined by
God and not free. But "if I am free with respect to action
A, then God does not *bring it about* or *cause it to be the
case* either that I take or that I refrain from this action;
he neither causes this to be so through the laws he establishes, nor by direct intervention, nor in any other way.
For if he *brings it about* or *causes it to be the case* that I
take A, then I am not free to *refrain* from A, in which case
I am not free with respect to A." Therefore God "cannot
actualize any state of affairs including the existence of
creatures who freely take some action or other."[4] Thus,
if "actualize" be understood in the strong sense, where
God actually brings about all states of affairs, and if the
possible state of affairs is one in which creatures freely
perform or fail to perform actions, then it is not the case
that God can cause or create free moral agents which
always do the right, and further this does not reflect negatively on his omnipotence since it would involve actualizing a self-contradictory state of affairs, i.e., a state of affairs in which God causes creatures freely to perform or
fail to perform A.

Suppose we understand "actualize" in the weak sense.
Here it might be supposed that God by his omniscience
would know what each possible being would do were he
created. Thus, in order to have a world populated by beings
which freely always did not sin or do evil, he would choose
for existence only those beings which he knew would freely always do the right. In this possible world it could be said
that God strongly actualizes the existence of certain beings and weakly actualizes their free choices not to do evil.

This view is also deficient, for two reasons. The first

we explored in Chapter 1. There we argued that such a view presupposes that God's knowledge includes counterfactual conditionals about the free choices and acts of actual or possible agents. According to this interpretation, God knows all the choices which all possible free beings would make and all the actions which all possible free beings would perform were they created, and on the basis of this knowledge he then chooses to create certain beings, i.e., those who always choose to do the good. But this then means that God knows states of affairs which not only will never occur, but are the possible results of free choices which never were or will be made. But in what sense can it be said that these possible states of affairs would be part of God's knowledge? To be such, counterfactual conditionals of free will must be true. But are they? They are not true by correspondence with any actual occurrence or state of affairs, for since they are counterfactuals there will be no actual occurrence or state of affairs so described. Neither are they true in that they are logically necessary, for they are contingent propositions, nor are they true in that they are causally necessary, for this is inconsistent with their being conditionals of free choice or action. Neither are they true in that they correspond with or follow from the possible person's character or intentions, for a person's character is not necessarily determinative of his action. In sum, counterfactual conditionals about free acts of actual or possible agents cannot be true and hence cannot be part of God's knowledge.[5] Consequently, weak actualization so viewed—where God knows all possible choices of all possible free beings and strongly actualizes only those who always do the good but only weakly actualizes their free choices not to do evil—is impossible.

Even if one holds the current view that a counterfactual is true "if and only if its antecedent is impossible, or its consequent is true in the world most similar to the actual in which its antecedent is,"[6] this does not alter the response, for it fails to show how God could know these counterfactuals in such a way that he could actualize a particular world based upon this knowledge. If counterfactuals of free choice are to be items of God's knowledge and if they are to be used in the selection of agents who always freely do the right, God must know them *before* there was an actual world and *before* he decided which possible world to actualize. But he cannot *know* them before this, since it is yet indeterminate which world he will actualize and which counterfactuals are true, for their truth depends upon the actual world in respect to similarity of relevant states of affairs. At the heart of this view there lies a fundamental circularity. The truth of these counterfactual conditionals depends upon there being a particular actual world, and which world is actual depends upon God's knowing all counterfactual conditionals and choosing to actualize that compossible set of beings which freely always choose the good (i.e., which world is actual depends upon the truth of the counterfactual conditionals).

A further problem arises for those who, like Plantinga, contend that, though agents make free will counterfactuals with true antecedents true (supposing that the class of counterfactuals be considered broadly to include such), there is no agent—human or divine—who makes free will counterfactuals with false antecedents true. They simply are true. But this is unsatisfactory, for since Plantinga holds that some of the latter are true in the actual world (if I were offered $50,000 for my tennis racket, I would sell it) while others are false (if I were President of the U.S., I would invade Albania), one wants to know why they are true rather than false or vice versa for any given possible world, and most importantly, for the actual world. As contingent, free will propositions, some agent must make them true; but as containing false antecedents, no agent can make them true

—an apparently contradictory consequence of predicating "true" of free will counterfactuals with false antecedents.

Secondly, even supposing that one could have knowledge of counterfactual conditionals of free will, the scenario proposed by this view raises serious questions concerning how one is to view the freedom of these created beings who freely always do the good. Suppose that I desire to purchase a photocopier. The salesman comes and demonstrates several models. One prints in color, another on both 8½ x 11 and 11 x 14 sheets of paper, and a third prints only on 11 x 14 sheets. Since I work in a firm which uses only legal-size paper, I decide to order and install the photocopier that prints only on 11 x 14 sheets of paper. Suppose, further, once I have my new copier installed, that I tell my secretary that my photocopier has the freedom to print 11 x 14 sheets of paper. She might argue in response (and disbelief) that this could hardly be so, since the machine can print nothing but 11 x 14 sheets of paper. But, I reply, that it can print only this size results from the fact that I strongly actualize this particular photocopier; if it did not print only 11 x 14 paper I would not have actualized it. Since I decided that this was the result I desired, however, this is the type of photocopier I strongly actualized in my office. However, I only weakly actualize the state of affairs which includes its always printing 11 x 14 sheets of paper; in this regard it is free.

Needless to say, something has proceeded amiss. Yet this case seems to be parallel in the relevant points with the case in which God strongly actualizes free beings who perform only the good. In both cases they are strongly actualized on the basis of knowledge of what the result will be and with the achievement of that result in mind. It might be replied, however, that the two cases are not parallel, for with the copier it is causally necessary that it print only 11 x 14 sheets of paper, whereas with the beings that always do right it is not causally necessary that they only always do right acts. That is, the photocopier is mechanically constructed so as to print only 11 x 14 sheets, whereas the beings which always do right are not mechanically determined to perform only the good. Thus, we could appropriately term the former determined and the latter free.

But granted this difference, is it a significant difference, significant enough to allow us to call these beings "free"? It would seem not. In the case of the copier, whether or not this particular copier produces 11 x 14 copies or not is really irrelevant; had it been such that it would have produced otherwise, it would not have been strongly actualized by me in the office; rather, I would have actualized another copier which produced the desired result. The result is necessary not because of this particular copier, but because this copier was preselected with achieving this specific result in mind. Similarly with the preselected agents which always do the good. Though they are not causally determined always to perform the good, yet this indeterminism is really irrelevant to determining whether they are truly free; had it been such that they would have chosen to do evil, it would have been the case that God would have known this and would not have actualized them. Again the result is necessary because these beings were preselected with achieving this specific result in mind. Thus, in effect, in both cases the result—a machine printing 11 x 14 sheets of paper or beings always doing the good—is necessary. Because the actualization was based upon preselection neither the actualized machine nor the actualized moral agents could do otherwise than they do. The basis of the preselection differs—causal determinism vs. foreknowledge of acts—but the actual results are necessary (could not have been otherwise) in both cases. And if necessary, the question arises whether it is appropriate to call these agents free. As it is counter-intuitive to predicate "free" of photocopiers so actualized, so it is likewise counter-intuitive to predicate "free" of beings so actualized. In short, even this concept of weak actualization—where beings are selected from among all possible beings on the grounds that they will always do the good—appears troublesome, for it seems to make nonsense out of the idea that these beings freely perform certain actions.

The atheologian might argue for a third possibility, namely, that God only weakly actualize any individual's actions but that he strongly actualize it that these beings are never confronted with choices or actions which are morally significant for them, i.e., choices or actions such that it would be morally right to choose or perform and morally wrong not to choose or perform, or vice versa. These individuals would then have the ability to do evil, they could do wrong, but they do not perform evil or the wrong because they are never afforded opportunity to do evil or wrong.

But in what sense is it said that they "can do wrong"? If there are no possible circumstances in which God would allow them to be faced with a morally significant choice and thus in effect not allow them to do wrong, what significance can be given to the statement that they can do wrong? Further, in that they are never confronted with morally significant choices, though they have no opportunity to do wrong, they have no opportunity to achieve moral good or be virtuous either. Thus individuals such as these would not be the moral agents necessary to satisfy P_1.

In conclusion: though it is logically possible that God create free moral agents who always do the good freely, it does not follow from this that God can bring it about that there is no moral evil. Whether there is moral evil depends on the acts of these free moral agents. Further, the atheologian cannot appeal to God's foreknowledge to guarantee a world without moral evil, for counterfactual conditionals of free will are not items of God's knowledge, and, even if they were, to actualize a world based on this knowledge would preclude us from ascribing freedom to the agents so created.

CAUSING AND BRINGING ABOUT

In a recent attempt to rescue Mackie's thesis, McCloskey contends that the theist's rebuttal rests on a confusion. He writes,

> [It] seems to confuse . . . the notion of "bringing about" with that of "causing." . . . To cause someone to act in a certain way, where the causality is incompatible with free choice, is very different from *bringing it about* that an individual acts in a certain way. . . . An able teacher will bring it about that his students become interested in the subject on which he is lecturing and even that some accept his conclusions. A host may bring it about that his guest drinks a cold glass of beer by placing one beside him on a hot day. And a girl may bring it about that a boy loses attention in a lecture by flirtatiously eyeing him. In none of these cases is the person affected *caused* to act as he does. . . . Compare the example of drinking of the beer, with the different example of the beer being put before an alcoholic who has been starved of alcohol. In the latter case I should be prepared to say that the host caused the man to drink the beer. Causing and bringing it about are different notions. We can bring about something by causing it to occur; but we can do so too without causing it. If pursued further, this issue would involve us in the question of whether reasons are causes. We need not proceed that far. The theists' notion of free will rests on a distinction between reasons and acting on reasons, and causes and acting as a result of causes.[7]

In short, McCloskey argues that though it is contradictory to say that God causes an agent freely always to do the good, it is not contradictory to say that God brings it about that an agent freely always does the good. It is possible for one agent to bring it about that another agent performs a certain action without overriding the latter's freedom.

Though McCloskey here argues that there is a difference between "causing P to do x" and "bringing it about that P does x," it is less than clear how he understands this distinction. One help toward specification of the difference is to be found in his examples. In his example of getting another to drink a beer, McCloskey contends that Q *causes* P to do x (drink the beer) when Q puts the beer before P, who is a thirsty alcoholic; whereas Q *brings it about* that R does x when Q puts the beer before R, who is a thirsty person. Apparently the difference between the two is not in what Q does per se—for in both cases Q does the same thing, i.e., puts the beer in front of the person—but rather in what Q does vis-à-vis P and R, and more specifically what impact that action has upon the choices of P and R with respect to that action. In the case of R, R is so positioned [environmentally and physiologically (e.g., not alcohol-dependent)] that though Q puts the beer before him, he can choose between drinking and not drinking it. That is, he has *reasons* to drink but the reasons (a beer placed next to him; a hot day; he is thirsty) are not determinative of his action; he could opt for not drinking (based upon other reasons). Here one could say that Q brought it about that R drank the beer by providing non-determinative reasons for his action. In the former case, however, P is so positioned that should Q put a beer before him he cannot resist drinking. That is, the environmental (a beer next to him) and physiological (alcohol dependency) conditions are sufficient to determine his action. Here one could say that Q caused P to drink the beer by placing it in front of him.

If this is what McCloskey has in mind, how is God to act to bring it about that free agent P does x but not cause P to do x? McCloskey's examples suggest that what is involved is some form of non-coercive persuasion, i.e., persuasion (implicit or explicit) which, when combined with the existing environmental and physiological conditions affecting P, is not sufficient to determine P's action, but yet provides P with strong (compelling?) reasons to do x.

But is this notion of persuasive power adequate to make Mackie's and McCloskey's case—i.e., that God could bring it about that all men freely always do the good, such that there is no moral evil? It would seem not, for if God's power is persuasive, giving compelling but not compulsive reasons for moral agents to do the good, there is no guarantee that God could persuade all men always to do the good. If it is to be a case of bringing it about that P does x, the reasons must be persuasive but not determinative; hence the possibility remains that the agent can choose to ignore the persuasively offered reasons and choose not to do the good. If it be argued that God's persuasion must ultimately be effective since he is omnipotent, then the persuasion has been carried to the point where it would be considered no longer non-determinative persuasion but irresistible coercion. But without this guarantee it does not follow from God's omnipotence and goodness that there will be no moral evil. Whether there is moral evil depends on the success of his persuasive activities, which cannot be guaranteed without making his persuasion coercive. In short, even were this distinction between "bringing about that" and "causing" sound, it would not rescue this objection against the above-developed criticism.

PERSUASION AND THE QUANTITY OF MORAL EVIL

It is at this point, I think, that the atheologian would turn to the inductive form of the argument from evil to make the following reply. Granted that God cannot bring it about that free agents always do the good, still it is the case that "less moral evil would have been compatible with free will or with the limited free will we are claimed now to possess."[8] In particular, God could be more persuasive for moral good. The amount, variety, and proliferation of moral evils make it obvious that God is not maximizing his persuasive powers for the good.

We have already shown in Chapter 2 that the atheologian has not made his case with respect to the inductive form of the argument from evil. He has not established that God is not maximally restraining evil, i.e., that there are instances of evil which God could have eliminated without losing a greater good or bringing about an equal or greater evil.

But suppose, for the sake of argument, we lay aside the conclusions of Chapter 2 to enable us to evaluate the claim that God could be more persuasive for moral good. We can now ask: How might God's persuasive activity be more effective with respect to moral evil? One possibility is that he could implant in us a greater awareness of the moral law, perhaps through an enhanced conscience, or he could enable us to have expanded knowledge, so that we might better know the moral law and the results of our moral actions. But such a response invokes the dubious doctrine that virtue is knowledge, that if we obtain more knowledge about the right so that we know the right, we will do the right. Wrongdoing, on this view, can be due only to our ignorance. But though knowledge may be necessary for virtue, it is not sufficient for it. Any such Socratic claim falls prey to Aristotle's objection, i.e., that it makes no allowance for weakness of will, lack of self-control, and the effect of the irrational on us.[9] Indeed, experience suggests that often there is no direct correlation between knowing what the right is and the doing of the right. Frequently our reason tells us the correct thing to do, counting the moral law as among its objects of knowledge, but we reject the advice of our reason and follow instead our emotions, passions, or personal inclinations to do something else, even possibly contrary to the dictates of reason. The will, as free, can choose to accept or reject the knowledge it has in determining its course of action.

A second possibility would be for God to give us additional reasons for doing the good. In particular, he could make it that doing the good would always be rewarded (e.g., accompanied by pleasure), whereas doing the evil would always be punished (e.g., accompanied by pain). This position, however, reduces morality to concern for advantage. That is, it reduces the ought to an is. Why ought I to do such and such? Because it will bring me certain desirable things or have advantageous consequences for me.

> When we are confronted with two men, one of whom loves justice, kindness and generosity, without thought for what they bring, while the other thinks only of what they bring, do we not want to say different things about them? Do we not want to say that only one of them loves justice while the other's love is a mere pretence, a façade? That this is so is shown by the fact that when the situation changes, when it no longer pays to be good, the man who pursued the virtues only for external reasons soon gives up his love of virtue. But, notice, even if the change in the situation never comes about, even if it always remains the case that it pays to be good, the difference between the two men remains unaltered, for what determines that difference is the relation within which they stand to the pursuit of virtue.[10]

In reducing moral considerations to consideration of advantage we have "falsified the character of moral considerations." What is commended is no longer morality itself or the virtues themselves but the advantage one can get from them. We are asked to do good because of what we get from it. But is it not the contention of morality that we should do the good because it is good?

A third possibility is suggested by McCloskey. He writes,

> Man is made with various desires, for food, drink, sexual satisfaction, desire to reproduce, . . . and the like. When hungry, we incline to eat; when thirsty to drink; when our lives are threatened we seek to protect ourselves; and so on. . . . This being so, the question arises whether God could not have made man with an inbuilt desire to be good, benevolent, to love his fellow man. If such desires were like our present desires, they would not deprive us of our freedom; they would simply bias us to the good whilst leaving the free choice as to what we shall do, to us.[11]

McCloskey is in good company with this suggestion, for even Aquinas suggests that God can incline our wills so that the resulting acts are certain, yet at the same time without necessitating them.[12]

Indeed this argument might be carried further in an ad hominem fashion to argue that orthodox Christian theism has often advocated precisely the opposite, namely, that all men have an inbuilt or inborn bias toward evil; men have evil dispositions, a corrupt nature. Yet this doctrine of original sin is not felt to be inconsistent with human free will. If the doctrine of original sin, which biases us toward doing evil, is not inconsistent with human free will, why could not God give us an inbuilt bias to do the good, a bias which was compatible with human free will?

Two replies to this thesis are possible. First, it might be queried whether the phrases "an inbuilt desire to be good" or "an inbuilt bias to the good" are meaningful. McCloskey compares this inbuilt desire with innate physiological desires for food, sex, and drink. But are moral desires comparable to these? Might it not be argued consistently that

moral desires—desires to be or do the good—are something that can be learned and developed only through human experience?

Secondly, suppose that it does make sense to suggest
that "an inbuilt desire to do good" is meaningful. From
the fact that man does not now appear to have such a desire, or if he does his desire appears significantly weak, it
does not follow that man never had this inbuilt desire or
that it was never stronger. According to the Augustinian
tradition, man originally possessed the strongest inclination to do the right consistent with his being morally free.
The first human beings were placed in an ideal setting
where they had daily communion with their creator and
were supplied with all their needs—a setting most con-
ducive to performing the right. Moral restrictions were
placed upon them, but these were few. However, in this
setting they chose to disobey God with respect to what he
required of them. Despite being placed in an advantageous
setting and possessing a strong inclination toward the good,
they freely chose evil. It should not be thought that a strong
inclination toward the good is a sufficient condition for
doing good, otherwise the view of freedom we have advocated—contra-deterministic freedom—is violated. Thus,
there is no conceptual roadblock to conceiving of the original members of the human species being so endowed and
yet choosing not to obey.[13] Finally, this failure by the earliest human beings has had consequences for succeeding
generations. The inclination to do what is right has become
weakened as a result of the evil actions of the first and succeeding members of the human species, such that "massive
moral evil could become commonplace in human experience." That is to say, though mankind was originally endowed with a strong inclination to do good, one consistent
with his freedom, the context of human action has now
been altered by man himself. "Once human beings com-

mitted evil acts the entire context of human decision and action changed significantly. The doctrine that attempts to spell out the nature of this change is that of original sin."[14] Though Augustine developed this notion ontologically, more recent advocates of this view suggest a more sociological interpretation. For example, the author just quoted enumerates three ways in which changes in the human situation followed from the sinful acts of the first (and subsequent) human beings. (*a*) Man now has bad examples to follow, whereas originally there were none. Thus, the context is not one which is entirely supportive of doing the right. (*b*) Not only must one think about opposing evil, but this opposition, if opted for, will itself bring one into conflict with those who advocate or perform the evil. "This will bring him into conflict with another human being, and as a consequence it may bring forth combative impulses that would not have arisen otherwise,"[15] combative impulses which can eventually lead to wrongdoing. (*c*) Those who commit evil will try to rationalize their wrongdoing to give the appearance that what they are doing is right. This rationalization not only will incline them to further rationalization, but will be communicated to their progeny. "Rationalizations of this sort are particularly influential on the young. Children who grow up constantly hearing rationalizations of misbehavior will probably accept them as the truth about right and wrong. If they are exposed not only to the rationalization but also to the truth, they will probably grow up confused and uncertain about right and wrong. Such error and confusion cannot but produce more moral evil."[16]

In short, the atheologian is correct in holding that man as he now is could be under other or stronger inclinations, inclinations which would encourage him to perform good rather than evil. What he is mistaken about is that mankind has always been in this condition and that were he not in this condition, he would not perform evil. The contention of the Augustinian is that man was originally in this superior condition, inclined to do good, but freely chose to do evil; the consequences of his and subsequent evil choices form the context in which human beings operate today. Man's present state is a result of previous morally significant actions. Thus, the existence of a good God, the original presence of inclinations to do the good, man's present weak inclination to do good (or strong inclination to do evil), and the existence of the amount of moral evil present in our world are consistent. "[E]ven if free human beings at one time had the strongest possible inclination to do what is right that is consistent with their being free, there is no reason for thinking that the amount of moral evil that has occurred in human history would have been any less than it has been."[17]

A fourth and final suggestion would be that God could be more "persuasive" by actually intervening in human affairs. In particular, God could intervene in the worst cases of moral evil, e.g., the mass slaughters of Hitler, the Khmer Rouge, or Idi Amin. Of course, this would be to limit human freedom, but human persons already possess limited freedom. God's sporadic intervention would not completely curtail their significant freedom. Human persons would be allowed to perform some morally significant actions, but insofar as the worst evils would be prevented there would be significantly less moral evil than there currently is in the actual world.

Furthermore, it is argued, this intervention is consistent with our own moral activity. When we see one person harming another, we are justified in acting so as to prevent the evil-inflicting action, even if our intervention results in limiting the freedom of the evildoer. Of course, we are not to dehumanize the offender, but we are justified in intervening in those cases where significant harm is being done to the innocent victim, and we are morally allowed to use adequate, freedom-restricting force to accomplish the protection of the innocent and prevention of the specific crime.

The suggestion advanced here by the atheologian utilizes the principle that if God is good he will intervene in miraculous fashion in human events so as to remove the worst moral evils. Failure to intervene is inconsistent with his goodness. But "the worst evils" is a comparative notion. Suppose that God removed all evils of 10^7 magnitude in our world. There would still be instances of "the worst evils" in our world, namely evils of 10^6 magnitude, and according to the principle advanced, God now would be under obligation to remove all evils of 10^6 magnitude. Were these removed, by the same argument the now worst evils (those of 10^5 magnitude) would have to be removed, and so on. In short, by consistently applying the principle that a good God is under obligation to intervene to remove the worst evils, we derive the consequence that God is required to remove all moral evils. But this would be to remove man's significant freedom, a position which we rejected previously as conflicting with P_1.

It is no reply to this argument to suggest that there is a point where the worst evils are not so bad (say, at 10^3 magnitude) and thus could be allowed by a good God. For an individual who knows only these evils, evils of 10^3 are the worst and would seem to argue against God's goodness or existence in the same way that the atheologian appeals to the worst evils humans experience today. He would not countenance the argument that since there are greatly worse evils conceivable, the present evils are not so bad and thus would not count against the goodness of God.

If the principle were modified to say that God must remove all evils consistent with there being human freedom and preserving the world as a theater for moral action, then it is being suggested that there is some line beyond which

God cannot remove moral evils. But where is that line to be located? Demarcating the line for this greatest possible miraculous intervention is difficult, if not impossible, for finite minds. Further, it is at least possible that the present state of affairs represents that point, that God already intervenes to prevent the worst evils to the maximal extent consistent with human freedom, preserving the world as a theater for moral action and development, and his purposes for the world and human beings. If this be true, then God already exercises maximal "persuasive" power.

The theist who opts for a free-will theodicy does not deny that God can and does intervene in human affairs. Indeed, he would hold that were God's restraining power over evil removed, there would be an exponential increase of evil in the world—a point we emphasized in Chapter 2. But he holds that God's action cannot be such as to violate P_1. That is, God's involvement will be consonant with the existence of significantly free moral agents and will be in the context of a world which allows for moral action and the development of moral character. This entails—as we shall argue in the next chapter—that it is unreasonable to conceive of a world operated by miraculous intervention so as to eliminate all or most evils. If P_1 is necessarily true, and if those moral agents choose evil—as apparently they do in substantial amounts—this evil does not count against God's goodness, though it does bespeak the present context of human action.

NOTES

1. J. L. Mackie, "Evil and Omnipotence," *Mind* 64, No. 254 (1955), 209.

2. H. J. McCloskey, *God and Evil* (The Hague: Nijhoff, 1974), p. 74.

3. Alvin Plantinga, *The Nature of Necessity* (London: Oxford University Press, 1974), p. 173.

4. Plantinga, pp. 171, 173.

5. Robert Adams, "Middle Knowledge and the Problem of Evil," *The American Philosophical Quarterly* 14, No. 2 (April 1977), 110–12.

6. Plantinga, p. 174.

7. McCloskey, pp. 120–21.

8. McCloskey, p. 119.

9. Aristotle. *Nicomachean Ethics*, Bk. VII.

10. D. Z. Phillips, *Death and Immortality* (New York: St. Martin's Press, 1970), p. 29.

11. McCloskey, p. 118.

12. Thomas Aquinas, *Summa contra Gentiles* III, chs. 88nn4 & 5; 94. We have considered this view of Aquinas in the previous chapter, note 14.

13. John Hick's difficulty with the account of the Fall (*Evil and the God of Love* [Glasgow: Collins, 1968], pp. 68–71, 314–16)—i.e., how could a being created good and in communion with God willfully disobey?—is based on several misunderstandings (though not of Augustine's position per se). First, he confuses the goodness which God saw in the created—a fitness to its ends—with moral goodness. That created man was declared by God to be good establishes the first but not the second sense of goodness. Though perhaps inclined to do the right, he was not *created morally good* (which is an impossible notion). Secondly, that the first human beings were susceptible to temptation—that they could feel and be aware of a power struggle between allegiance to God and self-assertion—is not inconsistent with attributing to them either a morally neutral freedom or an inclination to do the good. That they opted for one set of reasons rather than another does not entail anything about prior moral character, unless one holds that reasons are determinative of free action, which we rejected as contradictory above. Finally, Hick contends that "in order for there to be any impulse or temptation in this direction he must either be stupid to the point of being less than human, or else he must already be possessed by a pride that draws him into enmity against the Almighty" (p. 314). But this dilemma presupposes the doctrine that virtue is knowledge, that if we know what the right is we will do it, and as applied here if we know the full being of the omnipotent God we will obey him, which view we criticized above.

14. G. Stanley Kane, "The Free-Will Defense Defended," *New Scholasticism* 50 (August 1976), 339–40.

15. Kane, 441.

16. Kane, 442.

17. Kane, 437. In light of our reference to Aquinas above, it is worth noting that his response to this problem is substantially different from those considered here. He argues that since human beings are complex and live in a complex environment, they have both a multitude of diverse ends or goods to be achieved and a multitude of diverse means whereby they can achieve those ends. As such, neither a natural appetite for the

good nor a natural judgment regarding the means to achieve these goods would suffice to bring humans to the state of always choosing the good. A natural appetite—specifically, the will—is insufficient because though by its nature it inclines human beings to seek the good, it is unable to distinguish in the multiplicity of circumstances and conditions the ends which would constitute fitting or appropriate goods for particular contexts (*On the Virtues in General*, VI). Natural judgment—which deals with the means to achieving the goods aimed at by the will—likewise is insufficient, for here too humans encounter many diverse means for achieving the proper goods which are presented in and under diverse circumstances. Hence, both must be supplemented by the virtue of prudence, which is right judgment about the human good in singular actions. "Presupposing the good end from the will, prudence inquires about the ways through which this good can be procured and preserved" (VII).

Aquinas further inquires about the origin of the various virtues and notes that though some are infused by God, others are acquired by actions through the use of our natural powers. While the theological virtues of faith, hope, and love are infused, the virtues "which are in man as man, or in him as a citizen of an earthly commonwealth, do not exceed the faculty of human nature" and are acquired through his natural powers (IX). Such is the case with prudence.

But though this is the case, why could not prudence be an infused virtue, thus enabling human beings always to choose both the appropriate good and the fitting or appropriate means to achieve that good in particular situations? Aquinas suggests two conditions under which it is appropriate for God to infuse virtues: (1) where the end exceeds what human nature can naturally attain, and (2) where God wants to produce the effects of secondary causes without the action of the secondary causes themselves (*Summa Theologica* I–II, q.51, a.4). Since always choosing and doing the good might be considered a case where the end accords with man's happiness and perfection but at the same time exceeds man's natural abilities, it might be considered appropriate for God to infuse prudence into human beings so that, by this infusion, there would be less evil than there in fact is. This infusion of prudence would then provide a way by which God could be more persuasive for the good.

5

Theodicy for Natural Evils

WHEREAS MORAL EVILS are by far the most important of the two kinds of evils, in that they concern the substantial moral and social wrongs we commit against each other and ultimately against God and for which we are held morally accountable, it is natural evils which are the most difficult for the theodicist to explain or to reconcile with God's goodness. For the creationist, God has been and continues to be involved (intimately) with the world. It is he who conceived of its plan, destined its existents, and brought it into being by his word. Further, it is he who guided its evolution, so that in the created he might realize the purposes for which he created. But if God made and continues to work with the world, how is it possible to reconcile his perfect goodness with the apparently unwarranted and wanton suffering due to natural (i.e., non–human-purposed) causes which plagues human (and animal) existence? How can a God characterized by omnipotence, omniscience, and perfect goodness be directly or indirectly the cause of debilitating diseases such as cancer, arteriosclerosis, muscular dystrophy, poliomyelitis; natural disasters such as earthquakes, tidal waves, floods and tornadoes; inherent defects such as Down's syndrome, sickle-cell anemia, spina bifida; pain-causing animals, reptiles, and insects, such as grizzly bears, crocodiles, and tsetse flies; and a host of other evils, each naming his own? Here there is seemingly no intermediary of free beings onto whom we can shift the burden of responsibility;[1] God is directly responsible for the existence of the world, and depending on one's view directly or indirectly responsible for the outworking of the original creation.

NATURAL EVILS AS PUNISHMENT FOR WRONGDOING

Interestingly enough, one of the oldest attempted solutions to the problem of natural evil makes the denial of this last thesis—that there is no intermediary role for free beings— the critical core of its thesis. Natural evil, it is argued, comes as God's punishment for human wrongdoing. God is indeed the cause of pain and suffering, but they come as a manifestation not of malice but of his justice. Eliphaz, in analyzing the natural calamities of windstorms, fire, and boils which afflicted his friend Job, puts this theodicy as well as any.

> Think now, who that was innocent ever perished,
> or where were the upright cut off?
> As I have seen, those who plough iniquity
> and sow trouble reap the same.
> By the breath of God they perish,
> and by the blast of his anger they are consumed. . . .
> Behold, happy is the man whom God reproves;
> therefore despise not the chastening of the Almighty. . . .
> The wicked man writhes in pain all his days,
> through all the years that are laid up for the ruthless. . . .
> [D]istress and anguish terrify him;
> they prevail against him, like a king prepared for battle.
> Because he has stretched forth his hand against God,
> and bids defiance to the Almighty.[2]

This theodicy makes an appeal similar to that made in the previous chapter. With respect to moral evil, we argued that the fact that human persons acted as moral responsibility-assuming agents provided a theodicy for moral evils. Because human persons by virtue of being human persons are sometimes free to choose and act, they and not God are morally responsible for their moral actions. Here with respect to natural evil human persons again act as agents and likewise in a role which makes them morally responsible for the evil occasioned. But the roles of human persons are different in the two cases. In the former, human persons have the role of actually bringing about the moral evil in the world. Moral evils are products of their choices and free actions. In the latter case, however, human persons do not actually bring about the natural evil, but rather produce the occasion for it. That is, they have performed evil acts and in doing so deserve punishment. Pain and suffering arise as consequences of their acts insofar as the administration of punishment is warranted by their wrongdoing. But though human persons act in a different role in this case, moral responsibility for the pain and suffering still falls upon their shoulders; they are morally responsible for creating the situation which required or brought about the pain-inflicting punishment. When my son disobeys me and justice requires me to punish him for his actions, the moral responsibility for the punishment inflicted rests ultimately upon him; I function as the mediator of the pain-punishment, administering the pain and suffering justice requires. But the infliction of pain and suffering is not held to reflect negatively on my moral character; indeed, to the contrary, one might argue that if I am in a position of authority and responsibility, failure to administer punishment might reflect on my moral character because it would be a dereliction of my duty. The punishment is warranted by the wrongdoer's evil act, and hence falls to the account of the evildoer. Similarly with God. His infliction of punishment on human persons is warranted by their wrongful acts, such that the evil occasioned in the punishment falls to their account and not to his. Indeed, were he not to punish at all, his justice could be significantly questioned. Thus God directly or indirectly causes natural evils, but since these are punishments warranted by our wrongdoing, they are not incompatible with his perfect goodness. To the contrary, they are a manifestation of the justice aspect of his moral character. His justice and our evil acts provide a morally sufficient reason for natural evil.

Several objections can be raised against this theodicy. First, this view cannot account for the pain and suffering experienced by animals, for it is generally believed that animals have no moral consciousness and hence cannot be held morally accountable for their actions.

Secondly, and more importantly, "the distribution of disease and pain is in no obvious way related to the virtue of the persons afflicted."[3] Earthquakes, plagues, viruses, and toothaches seem to strike randomly, without reference to good and evil performances or moral character. The wall of water unleashed by the Rapid City, South Dakota, flood or the Toccoa, Georgia, dam burst did not select out the unjust to be drowned and bypass the just. The tsetse fly does not first discern the moral qualities of its potential victims. Physicians do not differentiate benign from malignant breast tumors by discovering the moral virtue or turpitude of their female patients.

It might be replied to this that though it is not obvious to us that there is any specific correlation between the victims of natural evil and their moral and immoral activities, this is due to the limitations of our knowledge; were we able to know what actions individuals have performed, were we able to have the wisdom and knowledge possessed by God, we would be able to see this correlation. This reply, however, instead of establishing what needs to be shown— that there is in fact a correlation between natural evils suffered and moral evils performed—assumes that this is the case. If any argument is provided at all, it is an appeal to ignorance.

Further problems arise concerning individuals born with

birth defects; surely it is difficult to maintain that these individuals sinned prior to their birth. Two responses, consistent with this type of theodicy, have been given to this objection. One finds them in a sense[4] summarized in the biblical account of Jesus' encounter with the man born blind. Jesus' disciples queried, "Rabbi, who sinned, this man or his parents, that he was born blind?"[5] Two possibilities—neither accepted by Jesus—are suggested here. The one is that the blind man's condition was the result of the actions of his parents. Jewish law and Rabbinic opinion were divided over whether the child might be punished for the wrongdoing of his parents. Some canonic passages (Ex. 20:5; 37:7; Num. 14:18; Deut. 5:9; Ps. 79:8; Isa. 65: 6–7) stated that the sins of the father could be visited on his children; others—fewer in number (Deut. 24:26; Ezek. 18:20)—opted for punishment meted out on the basis of individual wrongdoing. Clearly only the former, which adopts a communal or lineage approach to the analysis of moral actions, would provide any support for the thesis that birth defects are punishments for sin. Thus, acceptance of this theodicy (coupled with a denial of the preexistence of the human person) would require adoption of a view maintaining corporate responsibility for individual moral actions.

The other possibility suggested here—that the individual himself sinned at the time prior to birth—is more fully articulated in a different religious tradition. According to Vedantic Hinduism, persons undergo a series of reincarnations determined by the dictates of the law of karma. According to the law of karma, the condition in which one finds oneself in successive reincarnations, whether propitious or unfortunate or a mixture of both, depends upon the moral quality of the actions one performed in previous lives. Actions have consequences or fruits, which are then lived out in successive existences or until there is no more karma and reunification with Atman–Brahman can occur. These fruits follow naturally and necessarily from the action.

But if fruits follow naturally and necessarily from an individual's action, can these fruits or consequences be postponed until a subsequent reincarnation? It would seem that, as natural and necessary, they would follow from the action committed somewhat closely in time, not in the distant future. Further, how are these fruits administered? It is unlikely that the natural causal sequence would "preserve" them for such an extended period of time and then "see to it" that each atman (self) receives the appropriate or just consequences of the actions performed in a prior life. In short, some teleological administrator would be required.[6] That is, to make sense of the application of karmic law, the karmic view would have to be incorporated into some form of theistic reincarnationism. In fact, such an incorporation, by reintroducing the element of punishment administered by a deity for actions done in past lives, would remove the obvious difference between the Hindu and the punishment theses.[7]

A karmic reincarnationist theodicy faces at least four fundamental difficulties. First, there is a noticeable lack of solid evidence to support the contention that we have had prior existences. Though some persons have claimed to entertain recollections about previous lives, these persons are rare: most human persons have no such memories. Secondly, and more significantly, the theory is unverifiable. Awareness of personal identity between successive reincarnations is essential to verifying or validating the doctrine of karma. Without this awareness the individual has no way of ascertaining in general the truth of the karmic doctrine, for he cannot discover whether he is suffering the consequences of his own moral actions, as the doctrine of karma affirms, or whether his present human situation is merely a product of other, natural causes. That is, without awareness of personal identity there is no reason to think that my karmic action now will affect *me* rather than some-one else in the future, or that my present situation is a re-sult of *my* past actions and not those of another. But this awareness is precisely what is missing in almost all cases, for we do not have memories of past incarnations. Thus the karmic thesis can be nothing more than an unsupported dogma.

Thirdly, suppose it is reasonable to hold to the law of karma, that all action has its fruits or consequences, such that all evil actions bring forth pain and suffering in later lives. It is not so obvious that the converse of this is true, i.e., that all pain and suffering are due to previous actions. But it was to explain the diversity of circumstances and sit-uations into which sentient creatures are born and of events experienced during one's lifetime which affect one person propitiously and another adversely that the doctrine of karma was introduced. Since there appeared to be no ob-vious, prima facie connection between the good fortune of one individual and his personal worth, or between the ill fortune of another and his worth, it was postulated that there is a law which governs the kind of birth, qualities of character and temperament, and subsequent circum-stances that a person experiences—namely, the law of karma. But there are many instances of pain and suffering for which we can discern apparently sufficient contempo-rary causal conditions. For example, if a person picks your pocket or a drunken driver rear-ends your car on a city street, or if you get bitten by a rattlesnake while climbing a cliff, or your house, constructed in the river flood plain, is flooded, the cause for your suffering can be traced (in the first instances) to the moral agent acting as thief or drunk driver or (in the second instances) to the rattle-snake or the torrential rains caused by a stalled weather pattern. There seems no reason to include a deeper level of causal explanation, viz., evils you committed in your previous lives. The principle of parsimony would require nothing more than the obvious causal explanation in terms of the pickpocket, drunk driver, rattlesnake, and torrential rains.

But, the defender of karma might reply, why did he pick *your* pocket or hit *your* car or why did it bite *your* hand or flood *your* house, rather than another's? Is not this best explained by appealing to the law of karma, which declares that it is in recompense for past actions? Not necessarily. One might be able to provide an adequate explanation of the action of the pickpocket in terms of what appeared to him to be a substantial bulge in your pocket, or account for the action of the driver in terms of his being temporarily blinded or confused by the lights of approaching traffic. The fact that you groped for a handhold at the mouth of the rattlesnake's den, or that you constructed your house in the flood plain whereas your neighbor built on higher ground above that level provides a causally satisfactory reason. It seems, in many circumstances, otiose to appeal to previous lives as explanatory causal conditions.

Some defenders of the law of karma admit that not all pain and suffering are caused by previous evil actions. For example, some suggest that the law of karma applies only to instances of natural and not moral evil; others suggest that we should appeal to karma only when other explanations will not suffice. The first is unsatisfactory because not only are there many instances of natural evil for which the causally explanatory conditions are readily apparent and satisfying, but also in many cases of moral evil the victim might indeed legitimately question why he was the victim of the evildoer's action and not another, particularly in cases where the action of the evildoer appears to be random, as, for example, the sniper's random selection of targets. The second is unsatisfactory in that it uses the law of karma as a deus ex machina. In both cases those who qualify the law of karma in this fashion deprive the law of karma of its explanatory power, for it was precisely to account for and explain all instances of pain and suffering that it was introduced. If the law does not apply in this explanatory way to all instances of pain and suffering, the problem of evil is reintroduced, for we now have no way of knowing which evils are caused by prior evil actions (i.e., which are justified by being proportionate recompense) and which are not.

Fourthly and finally, the doctrine of karma is advanced on the ground that it is a powerful support for the objective moral law. It protects the objective moral order in that it necessitates proportionate recompense for evil actions and a correlative reward for good actions, and it asserts individual moral responsibility for the acts one performs in that recompense and reward must be personal. If the doctrine of karma is to have moral significance for us, however, one would expect that we would be (painfully) aware of the prior existences and past specific evils performed so that the proportionate, personal punishment might be effective for us and that we would not repeat the immoral actions. But since there is no recollection of our previous lives and their constituent actions, there can be in this present life no repentance for, feeling of moral accountability for, or rectification of the deeds done. The doctrine does not succeed in supporting the objective moral law if the past is unremembered and present acts requited in an unknown future embodiment which has no conscious connection with our present embodiment.

How shall we summarize our findings with respect to this penal theodicy? By now it should be apparent that a penal theodicy faces significant difficulties. Though this theodicy must be rejected as providing an overall reconciliation of natural evils with God's goodness, however, this is not to say that it does not explain some instances of natural evils. As we noted above, it is in character with God's justice that he mete out punishment for our sins, and punishment by its very nature is painful, not pleasant. Further, it is both reasonable and consistent with divine revelation to believe that God uses natural evils as a means of punishment in his administration of justice. Where the difficulty now lies, however, is attempting to decide which natural evils we suffer are meant to be punishments, and which require another explanation.

NATURAL EVILS AS NECESSARY MEANS TO THE GOOD

A second traditional theodicy contends that natural evils are necessary means to significant goods. This view is broached in both a religious-moral and a natural-physical guise. Under the religious-moral guise the contention of the theodicist is that natural evils are necessary to arouse people from religious apathy and lives of disobedience and uncaring and to inspire in them reverential awe for God and repentance for their sins. Human beings seemingly do not pay much attention to God unless and until something evil befalls them. Popularly put: people are like animals; they do not look up unless they are placed on their backs. As calls to repentance and allegiance to God, natural evils are means to the good, and hence instead of being feared or shunned they are to be welcomed as messages from God, informing us of our sinful condition.[8]

Natural evils are also seen as necessary to moral and spiritual growth, for it is only in reaction to difficulty that we develop moral character. Just as our muscles develop and strengthen only as they encounter resistance, so our virtues develop and mature only as we face hardships, temptation, frustration, and difficulty. "The divine purpose behind the world is one of soul-making. . . . The kind of goodness which . . . God desires in his creatures could not in fact be created except through a long process of creaturely experience in response to challenges and disciplines of various kinds."[9] Courage develops amid danger, perseverance in difficulty, honesty defying temptation, charity confronted with privation and need, self-sacrifice in the context of struggle, self-esteem in the face of challenge, confidence against uncertainty, love where obstacles abound. These virtues then are the greater good which necessitates the presence of natural evils. Apart from the presence of natural evils of some sort they cannot exist or be realized.

In the natural-physical guise, natural evils are held to be necessary means to certain goods in that they are nature's way of informing us that rectification of some sort is necessary. Pains and sufferings are biological and psychological warning signals, without which we would not know that something was amiss with our physical or psychological existence, that something must be corrected. The toothache tells us that bacteria are destroying our teeth and that a visit to the dentist is in order; the headache reminds us to relax our frantic pace of daily life. Sunburn warns us against the dangers of overexposure to the sun, while other burn sensations get us to drop dangerous, hot objects. Here again, insofar as natural evils are necessary means to good, they are justified by the greater good they promote.

As guises of a comprehensive theodicy, however, both are decidedly suspect. For one thing, in what sense are these evils *necessary* for attaining the goods to which they are the means? As argued in Chapter 1, evils of some sort are logically necessary to the attainment of certain moral virtues; but many of the goods described by this theodicy seemingly could be achieved without the presence or utilization of evil or painful means. In the theological case where evil is God's call to repentance it would seem that there are other means by which God could awaken us out of our sinful slumber and bring us to repentance; it would not seem necessary that God use pain and suffering. For example, God could speak to each individual by means of some miraculous special revelation, as he did with Balaam and Saul of Tarsus. In the natural-physical case where evil is nature's call to rectification, it would seem that there are other ways or systems which could be established to warn us concerning impending harm or lurking dangers. What this system might be like, however, is not so easy to determine. Hume argued[10] that it seems that pleasure motivates men as well as if not better than pain. Thus, a warning system consisting simply of diminished pleasure rather than pain might suffice. Alternatively, it might be suggested that a reward system might also be effective, since experiments suggest that reward functions as a more effective motivator than punishment. Hume's suggestion appears defective, however, for that "which is the pleasant or unpleasant quality of experiences, is relative and variable. A given experience does not have an absolute place on the hedonic scale. Its position consists in its relation to other experiences that are more pleasant or less pleasant than itself."[11] Consequently, the diminished pleasure would be considered evil and the absence of reward cause for suffering, such that the natural evils would not in fact have been eliminated by this system. The essential contrast between the pleasant and unpleasant remains. Granted this, though some evil (pain and suffering) might be necessary for the realization of the greater good, one still can legitimately wonder whether all natural evils present in our world are so necessary. For even if pain and suffering did constitute effective warning systems, this theodicy is still suspect, for though pain informs of arthritis, to what does the arthritic condition itself point? Though toothaches tell of tooth decay, the decay itself can hardly be considered a warning. In short, this theodicy might succeed in showing that some evils are necessary means to greater goods and as such might provide a justification for some of our pain, but much of our suffering (grief, despair, loneliness) and the diseased conditions themselves which the pain announces are left unaccounted for.

For another thing, in both the theological-moral and the natural-physical cases pain and suffering do not work very effectively. With respect to the religious-moral argument, it is true that some people do discover God in times of crisis and disaster. Yet the opposite also occurs—the apparent randomness and unjustified calamity of natural evils, their prevalence and intensity, can turn people away from God. "How can a good God allow a child to suffer from spina bifida or leukemia, or thousands to suffer homelessness and starvation from floods and earthquakes?" they query, with diminishing faith. Rather than inspiring reverence, awe, and repentance, natural calamities often bring defection from faith, which would be the opposite of what was intended.

Likewise the hardships and difficulties humans face often become too great, working to destroy rather than to build up the intended virtues. Temptations brought on by deprivation encourage dishonesty. Devastating disasters and diseases with unending pain occasion despair rather than courage. Must the privation and need be so great to invoke the virtue of human charity? As Hick writes, critiquing his own position,

> It is true that sometimes . . . there are sown or there come to flower even in the direst calamity graces of character that seem to make even that calamity itself worth while. A selfish spirit may be moved to compassion, a thoughtless person discover life's depths and be deepened thereby, a proud spirit learn pa-

tience and humility, a soft, self-indulgent character be made strong in the fires of adversity. All this may happen, and has happened. But it may also fail to happen, and instead of gain there may be sheer loss. Instead of ennobling, affliction may crush the character and wrest from it whatever virtues it possesses.[12]

Further, it often happens that the end of the suffering is death, before the virtues can be lived out and their fruits manifested. And indeed, some mentally and physically defective infants never achieve a level where they can learn and fashion their virtues.

If this be the reason for natural evil, it would seem that it is often ineffective and succeeds too infrequently to be ascribed to the divine plan. If the argument succeeds at all, it succeeds in rescuing God's perfect goodness at the high expense of his wisdom.

The natural-physical argument fares no better. It is frequently the case that pain comes too late, after the disease is well-established and the prospects are terminal, and it comes with an intensity often disproportionate to the illness. Thus, instead of functioning as an early-warning signal leading to the possibility of rectification of the ill, pain is frequently an excruciating companion through the final (and sometimes prolonged) stages of life, exacerbating the situation. Further, we must not view this pain-state from the perspective of our tranquilized and pain-killer–dosed society; these are relatively recent developments which until the advent of modern medicine were unavailable to human persons (and still are unavailable to much of the world's human and most of its animal inhabitants). Again this argument rescues God's perfect goodness at the high cost of his wisdom; surely a more effective and efficient and less painful warning system could have been devised, one which warned in the earliest stages when corrective action would be beneficial, or at least which, after warning for so long, could be turned off so the doomed arthritic could live with her affliction in peace.

As a comprehensive theodicy, then, its value and role are extremely limited: it accounts for some hardship in relation to developing virtues, for some pain for those who would not respond even to a direct revelation from God, for some warning pain but not for the diseases, calamities, or debilitating conditions which cause the pain.

ARGUMENT FROM NATURAL LAWS

Let us now attempt to construct a theodicy for natural evils which is more comprehensive in scope, i.e., an argument from natural laws which will provide a morally sufficient reason for all natural evils (or at least for those not accounted for by the above-proffered morally sufficient reasons). In general what I want to argue is that the natural evils which human persons (and animals) experience (by and large) are not willed by God, but are the consequences of the outworking upon sentient creatures of the natural laws according to which God's creation operates. This creation, in order to make possible the existence of moral agents (in this case, human persons), had to be ordered according to some set of natural laws. Consequently, the possibility arises that sentient creatures like ourselves can be negatively affected by the outworkings of these laws in nature, such that we experience pain, suffering, disability, disutility, and at times the frustration of our good desires. Since a world with free persons making choices between moral good and evil and choosing a significant amount of moral good is better than a world without free persons and moral good and evil, God in creating had to create a world which operated according to natural laws to achieve this higher good. Thus, his action of creation of a natural world and a natural order, along with the resulting pain and pleasure which we experience, is justified. The natural evils which afflict us—diseases, sickness, disasters, birth defects —are all the outworking of the natural system of which we are a part. They are the by-products made possible by that which is necessary for the greater good.

Before we develop this in more detail, let us recall the definitions and presuppositions spelled out in Chapter 3.

D_1 A being x is omnipotent if and only if it is capable of bringing about any contingent state of affairs (a) whose description does not contain or entail a contradiction, and (b) whose description does not exclude or entail the exclusion of x or any omnipotent agent from among those which may have brought about that state of affairs.

D_2 An action is morally significant for a given person at a given time if and only if it would be wrong for him to perform the action then but right to refrain, or vice versa.

D_3 A person is significantly free, on a given occasion, if he is then free either to perform or to refrain from performing an action that is morally significant for him.

D_4 A miracle is a special act of God whereby for a moral or spiritual purpose he produces in nature a new being or mode of being.

P_1 A world containing significantly free persons making choices between moral good and evil and choosing a significant amount of moral good is superior to a world lacking significantly free persons and moral good and evil.

P_2 For a person to be a moral agent, he must be at times significantly free.

P_3 No person can be held morally accountable for that which it is impossible for that person to have done otherwise.

P_4 Human persons are beings capable of morally significant actions.

With these definitions and presuppositions we can proceed to formulate an argument from natural laws. We can begin by noting that the possible worlds which God could have created divide into two classes. He could have created either a world which operates according to natural laws or one which he operates by miraculous intervention. A world which operates according to divine miraculous intervention, however, is not a viable alternative for God. To see this, let us explore what the consequences of such a world would be.

First, for everything that would occur, God would have to intervene to bring it about—and with respect to evil, bring it about such that the consequences were always propitious or pleasurable. Thus, in a world which operates according to divine miraculous intervention, there would be no necessary relation between phenomena, and in particular between cause and effect. In some instances one effect would follow from a certain set of conditions, another time a different effect, and so on, such that ultimately an uncountable variety of effects would follow a given set of conditions. There would be no regularity of sequence, no natural production of effects.

But without the regularity which results from the governance of natural laws, rational action would be impossible. Without regularity of sequence, agents could not entertain rational expectations, make predictions, estimate probabilities, or calculate prudence.[13] They would not be able to know what to expect about any course of action they would like to take. Whether or not such action would be possible, what they would have to do to have God bring it about, whether it could occur as they planned (supposing agents could plan, which is doubtful), what the consequences would be—all this would be unknown and unknowable. Hence, agents could not know or even suppose what course of action to take to accomplish a certain rationally conceived goal. Thus, rational agents could neither propose action nor act themselves.

But proposing action and acting on that proposal are

essential for an agent's determination as a moral being. "Good" is predicated of moral agents when proper intentions come to fruition in right conduct; "bad" when improper intentions result in wrong conduct. But since they would be unable to rationally conceive what actions to take in order to achieve certain goals, and since they could not perform the actions, a world operated by miracle would prevent moral agents from formulating or carrying out their moral intentions. In effect, it would become impossible for agents to be moral beings. In short,

> It cannot be too strongly insisted that a world which is to be a moral order must be a physical order characterised by law or regularity. The theist is only concerned to invoke the fact that law-abidingness . . . is an essential condition of the world being a theatre of moral life. Without such regularity in physical phenomena there could be no probability to guide us: no prediction, no prudence, no accumulation of ordered experience, no pursuit of premeditated ends, no formation of habit, no possibility of character or of culture. Our intellectual faculties could not have developed. . . . And without rationality, morality is impossible.[14]

But according to P_1 a world with moral agents is superior to a world lacking moral agents. But the existence of moral agents is incompatible with a world operated according to miracle. Therefore, to achieve the greater good God had to actualize a world operated by natural law.

Secondly, that a world operated by miracle is incompatible with the existence of moral agents, and hence is not a viable option for God to actualize, can be shown with reference to P_2, namely, that for an agent to be a moral agent he must at times be significantly free. To see this, let us introduce an instance of moral evil. Suppose that Delilah was approached by Philistine lords, who promised her great wealth if she would deprive Samson of his hair and thereby his strength. And suppose that not only did the thought of great wealth please Delilah, but likewise the thought that she would now be one up on Samson, who had repeatedly lied to her. In order successfully to deprive Samson of his powers, she entices him to her home and proceeds to put him to sleep with a drugged martini. But since the success of Delilah's scheme would bring unhappiness and suffering to Samson and enslavement to his countrymen, God would have to act in such a way that Delilah's plan to shave his head would not succeed. The drug would not work; the scissors would be too dull; Samson's hair would have unusual tensile strength; he wore a wig. Thus, though Delilah desired to deprive Samson of his hair and his strength, since it was an evil-occasioning act God would not bring it to pass, such that she could not do otherwise than not commit the evil act. Consequently, she would not be significantly free with respect to this morally significant act.

One could perhaps push this example even further, to wonder whether God could even allow Delilah to entertain such evil thoughts. To have this idea of depriving Samson of his hair, certain neurological processes are necessary. Hence, in a world operated by miracle God would have to be active in Delilah's brain states. Would not God have to prevent her from having this immoral idea in order to eliminate evil in the form of thoughts?

The consequence of this is plain: in a world operated by miracle and operated so as to prevent all evil, agents could not will evil, and even if they could, the evil which they willed could not be actualized. In such a world there would be no significantly free agents. Hence, a world run by divine miraculous intervention would be incompatible with a world inhabited by significantly free moral agents. Hence, granted the necessary truths P_1 and P_2, if God is to actualize the greater good in his creation, for him to actualize this option would be impossible.

Thirdly, a world operated by miracle would itself not solve the problem of evil. The very thing which would be good for or bring pleasure to one person might not be good for or bring pleasure to another. Returning to our example of Delilah and Samson, if God intervenes and brings Delilah's barbering actions to pass, then Delilah and the Philistines would be happy but Samson and the Israelites would be unhappy. If God intervenes not to actualize her barbering intentions, then Delilah and her consorts would be unhappy, while Samson and his countrymen would be happy. Hence an impossible situation results: God cannot both allow and prevent Samson's haircut simultaneously; to do so would be logically contradictory. Moreover, it would not do for God to allow Delilah to cut his hair and then miraculously restore it, for her intentions to deprive Samson of his hair and thereby his strength would still be frustrated. Hence, a world operated according to miracle could conceivably result in self-contradictory situations, if God is to eliminate all evil.

Returning to the argument from natural law, our first premise was that God could create a world which operated either according to natural laws or by divine miraculous intervention. But we have seen that a world run by miracle is incompatible with a world inhabited by moral agents. Therefore, God could not have created a world operated by divine miraculous intervention and inhabited by significantly free moral agents. Since P_1 is a necessary truth, for God to actualize the greater good it was necessary that the world he create operate according to natural law. But natural evils are a consequence of natural objects acting according to natural laws upon sentient, natural creatures; they are made possible by the existence of nature operating according to natural laws and of sentient persons. Since the greater good entails the possibility of natural evil and since according to P_3 an in-

dividual cannot be held morally accountable or blameworthy for that which it is impossible for him to have done
otherwise, God cannot be held morally accountable or
blameworthy for natural evils. Thus we have a morally
sufficient reason for the existence of natural evil.

OBJECTIONS

Several objections might be raised against this argument.
Let me note three of them. (1) First, does not this argument for the impossibility of a world operated by miraculous intervention limit God and consequently entail a denial of his omnipotence? The answer, I believe, is in the
negative. Above, we defined omnipotence as the capability
of bringing about that the description of which is not self-
contradictory or does not entail a contradiction or absurdity. But as we have seen a world operated by miracle and
inhabited by moral agents would entail a contradiction or
absurdity. Since P_1 is necessarily true, the impossibility
does not conflict with God's omnipotence.

(2) Secondly, is there not a middle ground between a
world operated by miraculous intervention and one operated by natural laws? Why are these the only alternatives?
Is there not a possible world which contains some miracle
and in which the remaining events are governed by natural
laws? In such a world God would intervene to prevent
natural evils, but in order to protect human freedom he
would allow moral evils to occur. This would negate our
appeal to the Delilah/Samson case. But what would such
a world be like? Presumably, a world which was only partially operated by miracle would be one in which God
would allow events at some times to follow a "regular pattern," and at other times not. That is, sometimes causal
conditions x and y would result in effect z, and at other
times they would be followed by an effect of a different sort.

For example, heavy snowfall in the mountains and collapse of snow walls will cause an avalanche to proceed down the mountain slope according to the law of gravity when no sentient creature is in its path; but should a climber be present, either that which causes the avalanche "regularly" will not have this effect this time, or the avalanche will still occur but will swerve around the climber or halt at his feet. But natural laws such as the law of gravity assert universal and necessary connections between phenomena. Then if events sometimes followed a "regular pattern" and sometimes not, there would be no natural laws regarding that particular event. But then the appeal to a "regular pattern" is specious, for "regular pattern" presupposes that there are normative natural laws which describe or govern the course of events, so that one can distinguish what is regular from what is irregular. "Regular pattern" has meaning only within the context of natural laws. Furthermore, if this absence of universal and necessary connections is widespread, as would seem to be required in order to prevent all natural evils, the world would have few if any natural laws; it would, in effect, be governed by miraculous intervention. Thus, though this so-called middle ground would remove the contradiction with respect to the possibility of human action vis-à-vis being free, the consequences of it still would be such as to make rational prediction and rational action impossible, and hence to make moral action impossible.

But is it the case that if we do not have natural laws we cannot make rational predictions? Is not general regularity enough to enable man to consider, rationally plan, and carry out an action, and hence be a moral being? As long as events happen in the majority of cases in a certain way, it would seem that this, coupled with God's non-intervention in instances involving moral evil, is enough to allow man to predict probabilities and make rational choices.

This objection is suspect in that it attempts to correlate two unknowns. It assumes both that we have some knowledge about the grounds of rational action in a world not governed by natural laws and that predictability is possible where there is only a generally regular pattern of events. It is true that as humans we entertain rational expectations, make predictions, and calculate rational action on the basis of mere regularity, on statistical probability. We do not experience uniformity and necessity. But this probability is itself based on the assumption that there are universal and necessary natural laws, that there is uniformity. It is a function of the fact that causes x and y always do result in z (either a specific state of affairs on the macroscopic level or one within a set range of limits on the subatomic level). But given a situation where there is only general regularity and no uniformity in the world, where there is no regular, necessary connection between specific causes and specific effects, in calculating action one would then have a statistical probability of a probability.

Moreover, our present statistical correlation of phenomena subsumable under natural laws is of a very high degree. Would a world in which God intervened to prevent natural evils contain this high degree of statistical correlation? That depends upon the answer one gives to the question concerning the frequency of instances of natural evils. But this too is an unknown of the objection. Indeed, here it seems that the atheologian wants to have it both ways. On the one hand, when first raising the objection against theism from the existence of natural evils, he points to the great amount of suffering and dysfunction in the human and animal world.[15] He invokes the great wastefulness of the evolutionary process, the frequency and debilitating effects of human and animal diseases, the devastating consequences of recurrent famines and drought, the excessively high number of mutants. On the other hand, in this objection to our solution he contends that the cases of natural evil are really few and insignificant, such that God could miraculously intervene in these cases without altering rational predictability. But the atheologian cannot have it both ways; either the cases of natural evil are few and insignificant and the problem of evil is not really a problem— such that the few cases of natural evils could be accounted for on the basis of such morally sufficient reasons as God's punishment for man's sinful actions or as necessary to realizing some higher good such as the higher moral virtues of courage, temperance, and charity—or they are numerous and significant, such that continuous divine miraculous intervention would make rational prediction and action impossible.

(3) Thirdly, could not God have created the world different from the way it now is in order to prevent or eliminate natural evils? This question can be taken in two ways. On the one hand, it might be suggested that suffering and dysfunction could have been prevented by the introduction of different natural laws. On the other, it might be suggested that these evils could have been eliminated by God's creation of a world occupied by different entities, e.g., one lacking poisons or parasites.

With regard to the former, this suggestion, though at first glance reasonable, under scrutiny can be seen to be absurd, for to introduce different natural laws would entail alteration of the objects governed by those laws. For example, what would it entail to alter the natural laws regarding digestion so that arsenic or other poisons would not negatively affect the human constitution? Would not either arsenic or the human physiological composition or both have to be altered such that they would, in effect, be different from the present objects which we now call arsenic or human digestive organs? To change the actual world sufficiently to eliminate natural evils, and therefore to instantiate a possible world with different natural laws, would necessarily entail a change in existing objects themselves. They would have to be different in some essential respects, such that with different essential properties they would become different things altogether. Fire would no longer burn or else many things would have to be by nature non-combustible; lightning would have to have a lower voltage or else a consistent repulsion from objects; wood would have to be penetrable so that limbs or trees would not injure. F. R. Tennant puts the issue admirably:

> To illustrate what is here meant: if water is to have the various properties in virtue of which it plays its beneficial part in the economy of the physical world and the life of mankind, it cannot at the same time lack its obnoxious capacity to drown us. The specific gravity of water is as much a necessary outcome of its ultimate constitution as its freezing point, or its thirst-quenching and cleansing functions. There cannot be assigned to any substance an arbitrarily selected group of qualities, from which all that ever may prove unfortunate to any sentient organism can be eliminated, especially if . . . the world . . . is to be a calculable cosmos.[16]

Thus, one cannot simply alter the natural laws without affecting the constituents of the world. Hence the first alternative reduces to the second.

The same reasoning applies to human beings. The introduction of different natural laws affecting human beings in order to prevent the frequent instances of natural evil would entail the alteration of human beings themselves. Human beings are sentient creatures of nature. As physiological beings they interact with Nature; they cause natural events and in turn are affected by natural events. Hence, insofar as humans are natural, sentient beings, constructed of the same substance as Nature and interacting with it, they will be affected in any natural system by lawful natural events. These events sometimes will be propitious and sometimes not. And insofar as man is essentially a conscious being, he will be aware of those events which are not propitious and which for him constitute evils. Therefore, to prevent natural evils from affecting man, man himself would have to be significantly changed, such that he would be no longer a sentient creature of nature.

But could God have made man non-physical? To answer this thoroughly would require us first to decide what is requisite for being human—a tall order which I do not here intend to fulfill. For our purposes, however, the contemporary response is fairly clear. Recent literature on the problem of personal identity abounds in affirmations of the Aristotelian notion that the physical is a necessary condition for being a human person.[17] The elimination of man's "animality" would be sufficient so to alter him as to prevent us from predicating "human" of that new being. If this is the case, then it is logically impossible to create *man* other than as a natural creature: if a being were so created, it would no longer be properly termed "human."

But, it might it objected, P_1 does not require that human beings exist, only that there be significantly free persons or agents. Agreed; but suppose that non-physical persons or agents were created. Even though these beings could not experience physical pain, as conscious beings they would be aware of themselves and their environment and hence capable of suffering. For example, the impositions of their finitude would be at least one source of natural evil for them. They could experience frustration, anxiety, intellectual limitations, and perhaps even mental dysfunctions. To eliminate this natural evil would require the elimination of the conscious aspect of these non-physical beings. But this would entail that they were no longer capable of being persons or choosing to perform moral actions. Since these consequences contradict P_1, this objection cannot be sustained.

With regard to the second alternative mentioned above, i.e., the suggestion that God could have created a world inhabited by different, non–pain-inducing entities, the way to bring this about would have been to alter the initial conditions, so that in the developing evolutionary process of the world according to natural laws, evil-producing beings would not have arisen. But to the suggestion that the initial conditions could have been different so as to eliminate natural evils, much of what we have just said applies. First, even with different initial and resulting contingent world-constituents, if humans (or personal agents) are physical beings and part of Nature, dynamically interacting with it, they will be affected in any natural system by the lawful events and physical conditions of that natural system. And it is reasonable to believe that these events and conditions will sometimes be propitious and sometimes not, and that humans (or conscious personal agents) will be aware of this. That is, though it is not necessary that humans experience natural evil, insofar as humans (or any personal agents) are natural beings it seems contingently true that any set of natural laws and conditions will be such as to affect them at times adversely.

Secondly, what would it entail to alter the initial conditions? If some scientists are correct, the universe has developed from the fiery explosion of a superdense mass of neutrons and photons, at temperatures of trillions of degrees. To have altered the initial conditions would have meant that the composition of this mass or of the constituent atomic elements that resulted from its explosion would have been different. But what the consequences of this would have been is impossible to know. Whether humans would have evolved but no infectious viruses or bacilli, or whether there would have resulted humans with worse and more painful diseases, or whether there would have been no conscious, moral beings at all, cannot be discerned.

Given a change in initial conditions, it is possible that this world would not have any less natural evil while not preserving moral activity. Therefore, this argument, which appeals to the unknown as evidence against the theist's argument, cannot be successful.

The atheologian might respond, however, that most theists see God more directly involved in the world by his creation of various components of the universe. Human beings are not a mere accidental result of a set of initial conditions and natural laws; they are special creations of God. But if God is involved in his creation more intimately via his creative activity, it seems that he could have not created or not allowed the evolution of such things as infectious viruses and plague bacilli. Granted the necessity of natural laws, God could interject new creations or correct evolutes at various times by his mere word, or have prevented the evolution of deadly and painful things.

But this would not eliminate *all* natural evils; the best it could accomplish is that some of the present suffering and dysfunction caused by, e.g., diseases might have not been. Yes, but would not a world without some of the more painful and debilitating diseases be a better world than the present one? Man himself can eliminate these diseases or introduce controls to prevent them from occurring, without apparent harm to the world or rational predictability. If man can improve his world by this achievement, why could not God either not have introduced these particular organisms into the world, or else have introduced other organisms to counter their activity? All men, for example, could have been born with an antipolio serum already in their blood. It would seem that the appeal to natural laws cannot account for all natural evils; indeed, the atheologian argues, I can conceive of a *better* world where there are fewer diseases, where pain-producing micro-organisms which man himself has eliminated or controlled by vaccines never were created by God. In short, the theodicist has failed to show that it is impossible for God to create a significantly better world with sentient beings, and that this impossibility does not conflict with divine omnipotence.

But though we have failed to do this, is the demand that the theist do this a reasonable one? Why must the theist show that it was impossible for God to create another and better set of natural laws to govern the world and moral agents, or to create another set of initial conditions which would result in less natural evil, or to inject different components at different times? Presumably because the atheologian can conceive of another world, run by natural law, with less evil. But can the atheologian really bring this off? What does he mean by "conceive of a better world"?

Note that it is not enough for the atheologian merely to say concerning a particular natural (non-humanly caused) event that he can conceive how it could have turned out better than it did, that he can conceive of another world exactly like this one where this particular event turned out for good rather than ill, for more than only one event is involved in conceiving of a changed state of affairs. An entire set of causal conditions will have to be altered for an effect different from that which did occur to result. Neither is it sufficient to state classes of improvements. For example, McCloskey writes, "We can describe a better world, with far fewer evils—for instance, a world in which beings were much more capable of experiencing pleasure of intellectual satisfaction or one in which there were no diseases."[18] These classes of improvements affect infinitely many other things, and perhaps for the worse. To follow up McCloskey's example, if there were no diseases, what would bring about the death of persons and animals, or is death also to be excluded? If so, overpopulation will certainly result. Further, what seem to us to be obvious improvements often have hidden costs. Microbes that were once thought best eliminated have been proved to have beneficial uses; insects once considered only destructive pests are discovered to be essential for plant germination or disease control.

If the atheologian is to conceive of a better world, what he must do, first, is develop other possible world-systems of natural laws and/or different components, and, secondly, show that a given *system* (not an event or class of events, but the system) would result in less evil than the present world-system. This project, rather than being flippantly affirmed as conceivable, seems quite impossible. But even if we grant that the atheologian could conceive of such a world-system, how would he commence to calculate the amount (quantity and quality) of evil which would result in that world? And how could he calculate the evil (quantity and quality) which exists in this world—not only now but conceived in its totality—and how could he ever total such up as to compare them? To do this would necessitate knowing all the implications of both natural systems, a task suited only for an omniscient mind.

Many critiques of theistic solutions to the problem of evil have rested precisely on this point. It is claimed that since, at this moment, I can conceive of a better state of affairs or a possible world without such suffering, God could (and by implication, should) have created that better world.[19] But it is not enough merely to conceive of particular instances which could be better than at present or classes of evils that could be eliminated; one must conceive of an *entire system* of natural laws and world-components which would have consequences, both individually and *in toto*, which would be superior to this world. But surely this is impossible. Hence the requirement that the theist show that it is impossible for God to create a significantly better world with sentient beings and that this impossibility does not conflict with divine omnipotence is not a reasonable requirement. If the atheologian cannot really conceive of a better world, the theist does not have to *show* that it was impossible for God to create a better set of world-constituents or natural laws, or even that this is the best of all possible worlds. Indeed, the last task is as impossible as the atheologian's attempt to conceive of a better possible world. All the theist need show is that a world which operates according to natural laws is a necessity if one is to have moral agents, which we have done.

CONCLUSION

It can be argued that in order to provide a morally sufficient reason for natural evil, the theist must show that God, in creating, could not have created a world other than that run by natural laws, and that this does not conflict with God's omnipotence. To do this we argued that there are two alternative world-constructions: a world operated by miracle and a world operated by natural laws. We have seen that a world operated by miracle is incompatible with a world inhabited by significantly free moral beings. Hence, assuming P_1, to realize the greater good it was impossible for God, in creating, to create a world which was not operated by natural laws. Further, since a world run by miracle would entail a contradiction with respect to the existence of moral agents, the impossibility of creating this world and realizing the greater good does not conflict with God's omnipotence. As such, we have a morally sufficient reason for natural evil.

Secondly, we did not, nor need we, attempt to show that the natural laws which govern our world make our world the best of all possible worlds. To do this, one would have to develop other possible world-systems, and show that these would result in more evil. This kind of project, it seems to me, is quite impossible. In like manner, we are free from the atheologian's charge that since he can conceive of a better state of affairs, this must not be the best possible world. This charge does not succeed because the atheologian has to do more than conceive of instances of less suffering; he must construct the proffered better system of world-constituents and natural laws and show what the complete entailments of both that one and the present world are with respect to natural evil. But this task is not one for less than an omniscient being.

NOTES

1. For a contrary affirmation, see Alvin Plantinga, *The Nature of Necessity* (London: Oxford University Press, 1974), pp. 191–93. However, Plantinga only suggests the possibility of natural evil-causing free beings (Satan and his cohorts), not the truth of any assertion about their existence.

2. Job 4:7–9; 5:17; 15:20, 24–25.

3. H. J. McCloskey, *God and Evil* (The Hague: Nijhoff, 1974), p. 91.

4. To what extent pre-existence of the human person beyond the fetal stage is suggested in the following passage is disputed. For a brief discussion of this see G. A. Cooke, *Book of Ezekiel* I, *International Critical Commentary* (New York: Scribner's, 1937), pp. 200–201.

5. John 9:2.

6. Indeed, this is the very claim of the orthodox school of Nyāya. For Udayana the karmic system provides one argument for the existence of a God who guides the dispensation of merit and demerit. See Sarvepalli Radhakrishnan and Charles Moore, edd., *A Sourcebook in Indian Philosophy* (Princeton: Princeton University Press, 1957), pp. 380–81.

7. Though the Vedantic view agrees with the penal theodicy under consideration in holding that natural evil is occasioned by the actions of human persons, such that moral responsibility for this evil falls upon these human persons, yet it differs from this theodicy in two important points. (1) Though it provides an explanation for natural evil, since it does not affirm the existence of a personal, loving, creative deity, the doctrine of karma does not and need not represent an attempt to reconcile the existence of natural evil with the goodness of a personal God. (2) Since strictly speaking karma is not deliberately or consciously imposed but is rather the natural consequence or outworking of a person's moral actions, it can be claimed that this theory is technically

not a theory of punishment. As Stanley Benn ("Punishment," *Encyclopedia of Philosophy*, VII [New York: Macmillan, 1967], 29) writes, "Characteristically punishment . . . is deliberately imposed, not just the natural consequence of a person's action (like a hang-over), and the unpleasantness is essential to it, not an accidental accompaniment to some other treatment (like the pain of the dentist's drill)." To some, however, this characterization imposes too narrow a view of the way punishment is administered; what is requisite is that the requiting be done according to strict laws or rules, and not whether the meting out is done naturally or by conscious volition.

8. The continuation of the biblical discourse noted above (Jn. 9:3) seems to point in this direction; Jesus replies to the disciples that the man was born blind so "that the works of God might be made manifest in him." Works of God are important in the Gospel of John because of their attestation of Jesus as the Son of God. They were performed so as to bring about the belief that Jesus and the Father are one, not simply as intellectual knowledge, but as leading to repentance (Jn. 10:37–38, 14:10).

9. John Hick, *Evil and the God of Love* (Glasgow: Collins, 1966), p. 344.

10. David Hume, *Dialogues Concerning Natural Religion* (New York: Hafner, 1948), pp. 73, 74.

11. Hick, p. 339.

12. Hick, pp. 366–67.

13. Ninian Smart, *Philosophers and Religious Truth* (New York: Macmillan, 1970), p. 169.

14. F. R. Tennant, *Philosophical Theology* II (Cambridge: Cambridge University Press, 1928), 199–200.

15. Hume, *Dialogues* X; H. J. McCloskey, "God and Evil," *The Philosophical Quarterly* 10 (1960), reprinted in Nelson Pike, ed., *God and Evil* (Englewood Cliffs, N.J.: Prentice-Hall, 1964), pp. 64, 67; Nelson Pike, "Hume on Evil," *The Philosophical Review* 72 (1963), reprinted in Pike, *God and Evil*, p. 100; John Wisdom, "God and Evil," *Mind* 44 (1935), 20; Edward Madden and Peter Hare, *Evil and the Concept of God* (Springfield, Ill.: Thomas, 1968), pp. 52, 56–57, 60, 63, 70.

16. Tennant, II, 201.

17. I have dealt with this issue in detail in my book *Is Man the Phoenix?: A Study of Immortality* (Grand Rapids: Eerdmans, 1978), chapters 4–6.

18. McCloskey, "God and Evil," 191.

19. As a case in point, I quote the following from Madden and Hare, pp. 54–55. "God could have created a world with somewhat different laws than the present ones which would have produced much the same

good results and avoided much of the gratuitous evil. God, for example, could have produced the same results in the biological world with the same mechanism of natural selection but without its present fantastic wastefulness. This could be done, e.g., by assuring a larger percentage of favorable mutations."

6

Must God Create the Best Possible World?

IN THE PREVIOUS CHAPTER I argued that it is impossible to show from experience that this is or is not the best of all possible worlds. The reason this is impossible from an empirical perspective is that it is ultimately impossible to construct the total world-system which would result in and from significantly altering certain undesirable physical structures or natural laws, or removing undesirable organisms or states of affairs, and to calculate and then compare the total values realizable in this possible world with the total values realized in the actual world. As such, from an empirical point of view, the theist is not required to demonstrate that this is the best of all possible worlds, or even to respond to contentions that the actual world is not the best *because* the atheologian purportedly can conceive of one better.

The issue concerning the best of all possible worlds, however, can be raised from a different perspective— i.e., not empirically but rather a priori. From the consideration of the properties or attributes which God is traditionally conceived to possess, i.e., perfect goodness, omnipotence, and omniscience, can it not be deduced that if he exists, he must create the best possible world?[1] That is, is failure to create the best possible world contradictory to God's possession of one or more of these traditionally ascribed properties or attributes?

One reply to this might be that there would be no contradiction involved provided that God had a morally sufficient reason for creating a world which was less than the best. But this reply is not adequate, for to say that God had a morally sufficient reason for creating a world less than the best as over against the best possible world is to say that ultimately it was morally better for God to create this less than best world than to create the best possible world. But this not only is a backhanded way of reaffirming that God had to create the best possible world, for if it is morally better for God to perform x than y, then x must be better than y; it also leads to a contradiction—namely, that the world which is less than the best is the best possible world.

The inadequacy of this approach suggests that the question remains whether God did or did not have to create the best possible world.

IS THE NOTION "BEST POSSIBLE WORLD" MEANINGFUL?

In undertaking to answer the question whether God must create the best of all possible worlds, we must begin at the point suggested by Leibniz, for, as he pointed out, it is sometimes the case that we use words or combinations of words to express an idea, and assume that since we can understand the individual words in the combination or recall using or someone else's having used these words, the words must be meaningful and the idea or ideas they express not contradictory. But "we cannot use a definition in an argument without first making sure that it is a *real* definition, or that it contains no contradiction. . . . We often think of impossible chimeras, for example of the highest degree of swiftness, of the greatest number. . . . It is therefore in this sense that we can say that there are true and false ideas according as the thing which is in question is possible or not."[2] Is the notion of the best possible world such a chimera?

Let us begin with the term "possible world." Following Plantinga, we can say that "a possible world is any possible state of affairs that is complete," and a state of affairs A is complete "if and only if for every state of affairs B, either A *includes* B or A *precludes* B."[3] Though this definition might be adequate in general, however, it is too broad for our particular purposes, for it is the case that we are inquiring not concerning possible worlds in general—which might or might not include God's existence—but concerning possible worlds with respect to the question whether God can and must create a particular one. Hence, for our purposes we will qualify this conception by limiting consideration to those possible worlds which are possible states of affairs that are complete and that include God's existence and his activity as the actualizer of that world. But even this contains an ambiguity in the word "actualize," for as we have pointed out in Chapter 4 there are two senses of actualize as applied to the activity of God. "In the strong sense, God can actualize only what he can cause to be actual," i.e., he strongly actualizes a given state of affairs S only if he causes it to be the case that S is actual. In the weak sense of actualize, God brings it about that something S happens if and only if there is another state of affairs which God has brought about, and God knows that if such a state of affairs is actual, then S will happen (be actual). In this sense God does not directly bring about all states of affairs; however, it is the case that he is responsible for causing or creating a certain being (person B) who then freely brings about a certain state of affairs S (writing with a pencil on his paper). Thus, it can be said that God permits or allows that state of affairs S to become actual insofar as he is the sufficient condition for the existence of the being who chooses to perform that action, knows what that being will do, and continues that person's existence.

Secondly, what is meant by "best" insofar as it is predicated of "possible world"? Several possibilities might be suggested. First, it might be contended that "best" refers to the kinds of beings which would populate any possible world. As such, a best possible world would be a world which would be inhabited only by the best kind or, if there were more than one best kind, kinds of beings.

To defend this thesis, it must be held that one can conceive of an absolute cosmic scale of being and goodness. That this is not only conceivable but actual has been held by numerous philosophers. For example, Augustine writes,

> Among all things which somehow exist and which can be distinguished from God who made them, those that live are ranked higher than those that do not, that is to say, those that have the power of reproduction or even of appetite are above those which lack this faculty. In that order of living things, the sentient are superior to the non-sentient, for example animals to trees. Among sentient beings, the intelligent are higher than the non-intelligent, as with men and cattle. Among the intelligent, the immortal are superior to the mortal, as angels to men. This is the hierarchy according to the order of nature.[5]

And Aquinas writes,

> The universe of creatures is more perfect if there are many grades of things than if there were but one. Now it befits the supreme good to make what is best. It was therefore fitting that God should make many grades of creatures.[6]

"Best" then can refer to the beings which occupy the highest rung on this cosmic scale. Applying this notion of "best" to "possible world," it might be argued that the best possible world would be one which was populated solely by the best created being or, supposing there is more than one, beings. Further, about this notion there appears to be nothing self-contradictory. That is, it seems meaningful to apply "best" so understood to "possible world" by saying that such a world would be one where there was only the best type of being in existence, i.e., that at the peak of the hierarchy of being and perfection.

In this thesis of a hierarchy of perfection in terms of a chain of being, however, there lies a hidden presupposition —namely, that this chain of being, as dealing with created beings, is finite. That is, there is an upper limit to the chain of being and perfection, such that there is among possible, created beings a best kind of being. Supposing that there are several members of this species of best kind of being, these beings would possess a variety of characteristics, sufficient to distinguish them from one another. But then is it not possible to say that the possession of certain characteristics by these beings is more preferable than the possession of certain other characteristics? Or cannot these characteristics, even if possessed by all the individuals of this highest kind of being, be possessed or actualized in varying degrees? For example, if, following the Christian tradition, one holds that at the top of the hierarchical chain of created beings reside the angels, one might follow Thomas Aquinas in holding that angels are able to know and consequently differ in their knowledge, and on this basis be able to distinguish between higher and lower angels.[7] But if this is the case, the chain of perfection is not finite, but rather infinite, insofar as it asymptotically approaches, e.g., the perfect knowledge of the creator. For any particular angel with n knowledge, one could conceive of another angel with $n+1$ knowledge.[8] And even if there were only one being, it would be possible to conceive of another being either with more characteristics or possessing characteristics had by that being more perfectly.

In short, one cannot speak about the best possible world simply in terms of the kinds of beings which populate it, for to have or form a hierarchy of being is to presuppose that there are characteristics which these beings possess or might possess which are different from each other or which various beings might possess in varying degrees, on the basis of which one could say that one being is better than another. But it is not obvious that there is a finite limit to the types of characteristics or the degree of their possession or actualization. To the contrary, these characteristics would exist or be possessed in an asymptotic series which increasingly approaches but never reaches the degree of perfection found in God. Thus, the notion of best possible world understood as referring to the kinds of beings which would populate it is meaningless, for the chain of being involves not merely beings, but their characteristics and the degree of possession or realization of these characteristics, and where there are degrees of possession or realization the chain is infinite.

Interestingly enough, whenever Christian theists have considered "best" as applied to "possible world" insofar as it relates to beings, they have not thought of a world populated solely by the best kind of being, but rather have argued that the best world would be one of richness and variety. For example, Augustine writes,

> What, however, is true is that there is a hierarchy of created realities, from earthly to heavenly, from visible to invisible, some being better than others, and that the very reason of their inequality is to make possible an existence for them all.[9]

And Aquinas, in addition to the passage quoted above, writes,

> Hence we must say that the distinction and multitude of things is from the intention of the first cause, who is God. For He brought things into being in order that His goodness might be communicated to creatures and be represented by them. And because His goodness could not be adequately represented by one creature alone, He produced many and diverse creatures. For goodness, which in God is simple and uniform, in crea-

tures is manifold and divided; and hence the whole universe together participates in the divine goodness more perfectly, and represents it better, than any given single creature.[10]

And finally Leibniz:

> Perfection is to be placed in form or variety; whence it follows that matter is not everywhere uniform, but is diversified by assuming different forms; otherwise, as much variety as possible would not be realized. . . . What we must say [is] that God makes the greatest number of things that he can.[11]

But even so understood, there is no finite limit to the degree of richness and variety that possible worlds could manifest. For even those who assume or conclude that the *present* world is the best possible world must admit that though "it contains an immense abundance of species, so that we are not at all inclined to complain of nature's poverty, yet it still does not by any means contain every possible form of life."[12] Between various life forms, whether actual or possible, there is possible an infinite variety of other life forms. And regarding the richness of the actual or any possible world, for any degree of richness n, there could be n+1 richness. In short, describing "best possible world" in terms of the variety and richness of the beings which would populate it does not make the notion meaningful, for again we come face to face with an infinite series of degrees of variety and richness.

A second interpretation of "best" as related to "possible world" would be in terms of "optimific." The best possible world would consist of those states of affairs which would maximize the sum total of utility, benefit, or good in the world.

What sorts of states of affairs are counted as the most beneficial or optimific? Hedonism suggests states of affairs which produce pleasure; utilitarianism suggests utility;

eudaemonism, happiness. Other possibilities would include the production of the most virtue, moral goodness, or good-will in the world. But no matter which of these be accepted, whether individually or in combination, as in the previous case one could imagine an infinite series of optimific states in which for any amount of optimific states of affairs n, one could conceive of $n+1$ optimific states of affairs, or considered qualitatively for any degree of optimificity in the world one could conceive of even more optimificity. For example, for any sum total of happiness n which might be produced, it would be possible to think of a greater total of happiness, $n+1$, which might have been produced. Thus, there could be no best possible world, since for any world which we would name there would always be another which was more optimific. Again, the notion of best possible world proves to be meaningless.

CONCLUSION

We have seen in the above discussion that there are substantial grounds for seriously doubting that the notion of the best possible world is meaningful. When we speak of best as relating to the created world, we find that there is not a finite series such that there could be a best possible being, state of affairs, or maximal state of affairs. Rather, we are faced with an infinite series of characteristics, degrees of their actualization, or optimific states of affairs, in which for any given being or state of affairs there could always be a better. Since the notion of the best possible world is not meaningful, it makes no sense to inquire whether God could or must create such a world; the very concept of such a world is indeed a chimera. In speaking of God's creative activity, the theist need only affirm with the writer of Genesis that what God created was good.

NOTES

1. Michael Quinn, "Mustn't God Create for the Best?" *The Journal of Critical Analysis* 5, No. 1 (July/Oct. 1973), 2–8.

2. G. W. Leibniz, *Leibniz Selections*, ed. Philip P. Wiener (New York: Scribner's, 1951), pp. 286, 324.

3. Alvin Plantinga, *God, Freedom, and Evil* (New York: Harper & Row, 1974), p. 36. See *The Nature of Necessity* (Oxford: Oxford University Press, 1974), p. 45.

4. Plantinga, *The Nature of Necessity*, p. 173.

5. Augustine, *City of God*, trans. Gerald Walsh et al. (Garden City, N.Y.: Doubleday, 1958), XI, 16.

6. Thomas Aquinas, *Summa contra Gentiles* II, trans. Anton Pegis (Garden City, N.Y.: Doubleday, 1955), 45n5. As this quote makes clear, Aquinas does not infer from the cosmic scale of gradations of being that the best world will be populated by the best beings, but rather by a divinely ordered richness and variety. We will consider this option below.

7. Thomas Aquinas, *Summa Theologica* I, q.55, a.3.

8. Of course, Aquinas did not distinguish angels in terms of the quantity of their knowledge, but rather in terms of the number of ideas and their generality.

9. Augustine, *City of God*, XI, 22.

10. Aquinas, *Summa Theologica* I, q.47, a.1.

11. Quoted in A. O. Lovejoy, *The Great Chain of Being* (New York: Harper & Row, 1936), p. 179.

12. John Hick, *Evil and the God of Love* (Glasgow: Collins, 1968), p. 85.

7

Why Is God Good?

IN OUR THIRD CHAPTER we advocated the following necessary truth:

> P₂ For a person to be a moral agent, he must be at times sig
> nificantly free.

That is, for a person to be a moral agent, he must be capable of making morally significant choices, where for him to do a certain action then would be morally right and not to do the action then would be morally wrong, or vice versa. Christian theists hold that God is a moral agent; indeed, God is the only perfectly good moral agent. If P₂ is a necessary truth, God must be significantly free, capable of making morally significant choices. But if God is capable of making morally significant choices, it is possible that he could do an action which is morally wrong. Consequently, it is theoretically possible to discern whether God is good based upon an evaluation of his transient acts.[1]

Yet, it is urged by most Christian theists that none of these conclusions can be true concerning God. God is free, but not so that it is possible that God could perform an action which is morally wrong. God is essentially good, and his good acts are an expression of this essential goodness. God's acts are free, but the goodness of his acts follows necessarily from the goodness of his nature. Consequently, it is impossible to question the goodness of God based upon an examination of his transient acts.[2] P₂ applies only to created moral agents and not to God.

The fact that these two different positions can be advanced by Christian theists suggests that attention must be directed to the question "Why is God good?" We shall explore two options: that God is good because of his nature, and that God is good because of his acts. Both options, as we shall see below, appear to lead to difficulties. Some have attempted to escape these difficulties by arguing that God's goodness is unknowable by finite, sinful man. Since I am of the opinion that this "unintelligibility thesis" has been shown elsewhere to be indefensible,[3] I want to direct my attention in this chapter to an analysis of two responses which assume that a meaningful answer can be given to the original question. I will defend the view that P_2 is a necessary truth, applicable to God as well as to human beings.

GOD IS GOOD BECAUSE OF HIS NATURE

The most frequently held view among Christian theists is that the statement "God is perfectly good" expresses a necessary truth, and it is necessarily true because by his very nature God is good. The classic defense of this position is found in Thomas Aquinas.

Aquinas presents two basic arguments to establish that God is good. First, he argues that God is good because of his being as Pure Act. Whatever exists has actuality by virtue of the fact that it is, and whatever has actuality is in some way perfect, for the lack present in its potentiality to exist has been overcome. Therefore everything that exists is in some way perfect. Further, since perfection implies goodness, all existents by virtue of the fact that they exist are good.[4]

But God is not like other beings; he is the only being which is self-sufficient and self-sustaining, in which being and essence are identical.[5] As the uncaused necessary being, no other being can affect his existence; he alone is the reason for his own existence. As self-sufficient, he lacks nothing. To put it in Aristotelian terms, he is the first principle and thus can possess no potentiality, for if the first principle has any potentiality in it, there is nothing which could actualize that potentiality.[6] God, then, participates in his being fully; he is most actual. Since perfection signifies absence of lack, and since he lacks nothing, God has all the perfection of being: he is most perfect.[7] In short, God is perfectly good because of who he is—the self-sufficient being whose essence is to exist fully and completely.

Aquinas' second argument for God's goodness commences from God's desirableness. He takes from Aristotle the view that goodness consists in desirableness: "the good is that at which all things aim." An agent is desirable by its effect in that the effect desires to participate in the agent's likeness. Now, God is the first producing cause of all things. Therefore, since all effects seek after God as their end, in that all things desire their own perfection, which is the "likeness of divine perfection," God is desirable and hence good.[8] In short, everything moves toward an end, and that end is God. Since the good is that which all seek, and since God their creator is that end, God is good insofar as he is both the efficient and the final cause of all things.[9]

For Aquinas, however, these are not really two different arguments, but part and parcel of the same argument. This can be seen in his argument for the denotative identity of goodness and being. All good is coextensive with being-desirable. All being-desirable is coextensive with perfection. All perfection is coextensive with act, and all act is coextensive with being. Therefore all good is coextensive with being. That is, goodness and being are the same reality; there is not a real but only a conceptual distinction between goodness and being. Goodness is being considered as appetible.[10]

If sound, Aquinas' argument establishes two points of importance for our discussion. First, insofar as God is good by virtue of his nature, goodness belongs to God's very essence: God is good essentially and necessarily. This follows from both of his arguments for God's goodness. It follows from the first argument because, according to Aquinas, God's essence is to exist. Therefore, the perfection of being, and consequently goodness, is part of his very essence. According to the second argument, God is the end of all things, including himself. But willing his own being is not done adventitiously; indeed, according to Aquinas, it is the only thing which God wills necessarily. God necessarily promotes the good, which is himself. What he has created likewise necessarily serves this same end in that it necessarily seeks its own perfection.[11] Therefore, desirability, and consequently goodness, are essential features of God's being. In short, goodness is not something which God merely happens to possess; it is something which he possesses necessarily. He cannot ever not be good.[12]

This leads to the second point: Whatever God does, since his acts must accord with his nature, must be good. Thus Aquinas writes, "God cannot do anything except that which, if He did it, would be suitable and just."[13]

GOODNESS AND MORALLY SIGNIFICANT FREEDOM

What is to be said about this particular view of divine goodness? More particularly, when "good" is predicated of God on the basis of his being, is "good" predicated in any meaningful *ethical* sense? What is involved in predicating moral good of a person? I do not propose to develop all the necessary and sufficient conditions but will focus on those necessary conditions germane to our discussion. A minimum condition is that the actions of the individual be right or good actions (whatever the standard of right might be). Further, good predicated ethically of persons seems to be incompatible with the necessary performance of actions; only if a person is free either to perform or to refrain from

performing an action can that person be held morally accountable or deemed morally praiseworthy for that action.
For example, we make no commendation of a man for not
beating his wife when he is in Detroit and she in Minneap-
olis, i.e., where the necessity is external. Neither do we
morally condemn someone if as the result of an epileptic
seizure she causes injury to another individual; here the
necessity is internal insofar as it is a feature of her genetic
or physiological composition. In both of these cases, since
the action was not done or done out of necessity, though
the action be right or wrong in terms of some ethical norm,
the agent who performed the action is neither praiseworthy
nor blameworthy on account of it.[14]

However, the nature of this freedom must be more closely specified. If it is logically impossible for any action that
the individual can perform to be a wrong action (that is to
say, if the only acts he can possibly perform are right acts),
then despite the fact that that individual is free to perform
a variety of acts, each one of which accords with the ethical
standard for a right action, it would seem not only inappropriate but impossible morally to commend him for
performing any of those actions. The reason for this is
that though the individual is free with respect to performing or refraining from performing any given action, he is
not free with respect to the *rightness* of that action. With
respect to rightness, he cannot do other than he did; it is
logically necessary that what he does is right. But then
what ethical significance can there be to his "choosing the
right" or "doing the right"? Since he is not free to choose
or do anything other than the right, moral commendation
becomes both inappropriate and impossible.

To put it another way, we are reaffirming P_2: For a person to be a moral agent, he must be significantly free. That
is, to predicate ethical "good" of a person, to say that
that person is morally praiseworthy, necessitates not only

that that person perform right actions and be free with respect to those actions, but also that he at times be free with respect to actions which are morally significant for him. Only if a person is significantly free, i.e., free *qua* the rightness of some given actions, can we then properly predicate good in a moral sense of that person.

Let us apply this analysis to God. On the view under consideration, God's actions accord with his nature, which is essentially and necessarily good. Since he cannot do anything which is contrary to his nature, it would seem that his actions necessarily meet the first necessary condition. It should be noted, however, that the fact that God in all his acts does what is good is not established empirically by analyzing and evaluating his acts but is a deductive conclusion from God's nature. That his acts are good is not a contingent but a necessary truth. Though this is the case irrespective of the ontological status of the moral standard, the status of this claim is most striking if, as Aquinas and most Christian theists claim, God's very nature itself provides the ethical standard, for on this view it is tautologous to say that God's acts accord with the ethical norm, for this is merely to say that God's acts (which necessarily accord with and cannot contradict his nature) accord with and cannot contradict his nature.[15] (We shall have more to say about the status of the ethical norm below.)

As to the second condition, God is free in that, on the one hand, he can choose either to perform or to refrain from performing any action (other than loving himself [willing his own good]); there is no necessity that he act transiently. On the other hand, if God decides to act, he can choose between various courses of action. Aquinas writes, "God's will is indifferent to this or that, since it is not fixed to one object. For he is able either to do a thing or not to do it, to do this or to do that."[16]

But what about the third condition? Aquinas continues,

"Yet it does not follow that in either case he can do ill, which is to sin." That is, though God is free either to act or not to act at all, or to choose between various courses of action, he is not free to choose between actions in respect to their rightness or wrongness. Once he decides to act, the only actions he can perform are right actions. It is not simply that his performances happen to be right actions; it is logically necessary that they be right actions. His actions then are not free *qua* rightness. But as we have argued, to predicate good of a person in any ethically meaningful sense, the person must be significantly free, i.e., capable of performing a morally significant action. Since on this view God is incapable of performing a morally significant action and hence not significantly free, good cannot be predicated of God in an ethical or morally significant sense.

One might reply that though ascription of moral goodness to human persons requires that the individual be significantly free, this is not the case with respect to God. The criteria for moral good which apply to other persons need not apply to the divine person. God need not be significantly free to be good; he only needs to be. Three comments appertain to this reply. First, if God need not meet all the criteria for moral good, which criteria must he meet and how do we discover which criteria are to be met and which dispensed with? Secondly, if it is not necessary that God meet the criteria of good as applied to other persons, then good as applied to God means something different from good as applied to other persons. Aquinas admits this, though he attempts to avoid the unintelligibility thesis at this point by appealing to an analogical relationship between God's goodness and man's goodness. Whether he succeeds in avoiding the unintelligibility thesis will not be pursued here, as it would take us too far afield into the doctrine of analogy, but it should be noted that some univocal predicates are necessary to get the doctrine of analogy off the ground. Indeed, the argument presented in the first section seems to proceed employing terms univocally. Thirdly, granted that good as applied to God has an analogical relation to the term as applied to other persons, the question remains whether the good analogically predicated on the *basis* of God's being is moral goodness. In the arguments presented in the first section above it was argued that potency is the source of imperfection; God as Pure Act has no potency and hence lacks nothing. But though not possessing the lack characteristic of potency might be seen to establish ontological perfection, it remains to be shown that this perfection includes or entails moral perfection. For Aquinas the connecting link is his contention that the good is being insofar as it is appetible or desirable. However, so conceived there is still no reason to think that the goodness thereby ascribed to God as the end everything desires is moral goodness. It is the goodness of being desirable, but it is not the goodness of desiring the desirable. The difference between these can be seen in the fact that the former is the goodness which any object—conscious or unconscious, animate or inanimate—might possess by virtue of being what it is (having certain characteristics or properties) or by virtue of existing; but one would not predicate moral goodness of unconscious or inanimate beings which are good in this sense. For example, a fresh strawberry pie is good in virtue of its being, and of course ranks higher on the scale of goodness and being as its properties are perfected: superior flakiness of its crust, perfect ripeness of its strawberries, appetible redness of color. But one would be wrong to predicate moral goodness of the pie; and should one declare that it is morally good because it exists and possesses these good (appetible) properties, that it has moral perfection because of (and in proportion to) its ontological perfection, one would be guilty of equivocation on "good" and "perfect." To reply that these terms are used equivocally when so applied to created beings but not when applied to God is again to force us in the direction of an agnosticism regarding what these predicates mean when applied to God.

In sum, if God's goodness is predicated on the basis of his nature, then the notion of good as applied to God loses its ethical dimension. Of course, one still can call God good, but good will have to do with the manner in which he possesses his ontological properties (i.e., he possesses his ontological properties perfectly) or in that he is the final cause of all creation. And as we have seen, it can be reasonably argued that Aquinas' arguments given in the previous section really serve to establish this kind of ontological goodness rather than moral goodness.

Furthermore, if our thesis be correct that good predicated of God on the basis of his nature is not moral but ontological good, then the ground for the response to the first condition for predicating moral good of persons stated above (that God's acts are good because their goodness necessarily accords with his nature) no longer suffices, for then equivocation occurs in that a non-moral notion of good as applied to God's nature is used to establish the fact that the goodness of all his contingent acts is necessary. That God acts rightly can no longer be a deductive conclusion or a necessary truth. It also follows from this thesis that the appeal to God's nature as the foundation of his will, which was used to escape the dilemmas mentioned in note 15, fails, for then the very same equivocation occurs in that a non-moral notion of good is used to establish or ground God's moral will.

In short, good can be meaningfully predicated of God on the basis of his nature, but the good so predicated is not moral good.

GOD IS GOOD BECAUSE HE DOES
AND IS DISPOSED TO DO THE GOOD

This brings us to the second view of God's goodness: God is good because he does good acts, and he is perfectly good because he always does and is disposed to do the good. The statement "God is perfectly good" is not necessarily true; God does not will the good necessarily. Rather, he freely wills to do the good, and could, if he so chose,[17] do that which is evil.[18] What then makes him worthy of our praise and worship is not that he does what he has to but that he does and has a disposition to do what is right.[19]

That God is able to do evil and that his choice in some cases is between doing good and doing evil does not entail that at any moment God might do evil. To say that God can do evil (he is able to do evil) is compatible with saying that God cannot do evil (it is unthinkable that he would do evil, given his virtuous character).[20] The "cannot" in the latter case, however, must not be understood as having logical force, as in the view of divine goodness previously considered. What force does it then have? Perhaps the following illustration will help. Suppose an attractive woman becomes enamored of me and presents a situation where I am encouraged to be unfaithful to my wife. In this case I have the choice between committing adultery and not committing it. That a choice is presented to me, however, and that I am physically capable of performing the act do not entail that I might commit adultery with her. To the contrary, committing adultery might be so abhorrent to me, to my character, way of thinking, and moral code, that it is appropriate to say that I cannot commit it. For example, I might say, "No matter what she does, I just cannot bring myself to commit adultery." The "cannot" here does not possess logical force; it is not self-contradictory for me to

perform the deed. Neither is it the "cannot" of physical inability or impotence, nor the consequence of the absence
of a morally significant choice in the situation. Rather,
the "cannot" derives from my character and disposition—
the act of committing adultery is so contrary to my person
that there is no real possibility that I would do it. The choice
and temptation are real, but my wife can be assured that I
will not succumb to the temptation. Similarly (though to
a greater extent) with God. It is not that he logically cannot do evil or is impotent or is not faced with a morally
significant choice, but rather that his character and disposition are such that doing evil is so totally repugnant to
him that he cannot do it.

OBJECTIONS AND REPLIES

Four objections to this view can be suggested. First, we
have granted that if it is only a logically contingent matter
that God is morally perfect, then it is *logically* possible
that he deviate from the moral law (though as we argued
above, there is another sense in which he cannot do so,
i.e., he is strongly disposed not to do so). But then, the
objector argues, if he did deviate from the moral law, he
would not be perfect and hence not be God. Therefore,
it must be logically impossible for God to do wrong.

The conclusion of the argument, however, does not follow, for the argument trades on an ambiguity regarding
the term "God." "God" can be used either as a proper name
or as a title. As a proper name, "God" names a particular
being. As a title, "God" is "used to mark a certain position
or value status as does, e.g., 'Caesar' in the sentence 'Ha-
drian is Caesar.' . . . To affirm of some individual that He
is God is to affirm that that individual occupies some special position (e.g. that He is Ruler of the Universe) or
that that individual has some special value-status (e.g.

that He is a being a greater than which cannot be conceived)."[21] If "God" is used as a proper name, then on the view just advocated "God is perfectly good" expresses a logically contingent truth. If, as the critic's argument hypothesizes, God did evil, what follows from this is not that he would not be God (which is to use "God" as a title) but that he would not be an appropriate object of religious worship. Thus, the above argument should read: "If God did deviate from the moral law, he would not be perfect and hence not be an adequate object of religious worship. If God is to be an adequate object of religious worship, he cannot do wrong." But it does not follow that it is logically impossible that God do wrong. What follows is that it is logically impossible for God to do wrong and to be an adequate object of religious worship.

If, on the other hand, "God" is used as a title, then "God is perfectly good" expresses a necessary truth; that is, one cannot possess the title "God" without being perfectly good. However, that any being X (e.g., Yahweh) is God is a contingent matter. Thus, though "if X is God, X is perfectly good" expresses a necessary truth, "X is perfectly good" expresses a contingent truth. What follows from the critic's argument is not that it is logically impossible that X deviate from the moral law, but that should it deviate it would no longer merit the title "God." Therefore, to bear the title "God," it is impossible that the being deviate from the moral law; one cannot be God without being morally perfect. But it does not follow from this that it is logically impossible that X (e.g., Yahweh) do wrong. What follows is that it is logically impossible for it to do wrong and be God.

The second objection arises as follows. It would seem to follow from the view under consideration that there must be a standard of good which is independent of God and according to which God's transient acts can be evaluated.

God's actions would then be deemed good or praiseworthy insofar as they met this standard and morally reprehensible if at any time they failed to meet it. But, it is objected, how can there be a standard of good to which God is subject? This would be to elevate something above God to which he is morally accountable. Karl Barth writes,

> For the man who . . . thinks that he knows a general principle which is actually superior to the origin and aim of theological-ethical enquiry and reply, and who in the matter of the doctrine of God thinks that he can actually step forward as judge in the question of truth, a theological ethic [one which makes the command of God the standard of good] . . . will necessarily be an objectionable undertaking. . . . And theological ethics on its part will cease to be what it is, if it dares to free itself from this offensiveness, if it dares to submit to a general principle, to let itself be measured by it and adjust to it.[22]

For Barth, the command of God is not founded on any other command or "higher" standard, "and cannot therefore be derived from any other, or measured by any other, or have its validity tested by any other."[23]

Barth likens the subjection of God's command to general ethical principles to the Israelite failure to obliterate the Canaanites in their invasion of the Promised Land. In tolerating Canaanite practices, they yoked themselves with the incompatible.

> This means that theological ethics has to accept the fact that it must not believe in the possibility and reality of a general moral enquiry and reply which are originally and ultimately independent of the grace and command of God, which are not touched or affected by them and to that extent stand inflexible and inviolate in themselves. It has to accept the fact that it must believe in the work and revelation of the grace of God alone and therefore in the actual overlordship of God's command over the whole realm of ethical problems. . . . Therefore, when it turns to this general moral enquiry and reply,

it will do so with the understanding that it has its origin and meaning from the divine command which objectively applies to man. . . .[24]

Divine command and action cannot be subjected to evaluation by any general ethical principle.

The question whether the moral standard must ultimately have its origin in the creative power and elective activity of God has a parallel. Many theologians and philosophers, the present one included, believe that God's actions follow or proceed according to the laws or principles of logic. For example, God cannot perform actions which are self-contradictory (square the circle or now make the past not have happened). But then are the laws of logic independent of God?

The above critics like Karl Barth respond in the negative, arguing that the laws of logic—in particular the law of non-contradiction—are not independent of God but ultimately are based on his nature or will. "The real and effective limit of the possible is the one which God has imposed on Himself and therefore on the world and on us. . . . If it is based merely on itself, it has no true basis."[25] "The limit of the possible is not, therefore, self-contradiction, but contradiction of God. It is not the impossible by definition, but that which has no basis in God and therefore no basis at all because it was not created by God."[26] "Up to and including the statement that two and two make four, these do not have their value and truth and validity in themselves or in a permanent metaphysical or logical or mathematical system which is 'absolute' in itself, i.e. independently of God's freedom and will and decision. They have their value and truth and validity by the freedom and will and decision of God as the Creator of all creaturely powers."[27]

What is unclear from Barth's discussion is the ultimate basis for the law of non-contradiction. Is it God's free will

by which he determines things, or is it God's essential nature? At times, he seems to regard it to be the former, as
in the last quotation above. Here the limit of the possible
depends upon God's free choice and decision. But then
whatever God willed—including that two plus two equals
five—would be the standard.

Barth accepts the idea that God cannot make this proposition true by divine fiat,[28] and his grounds for saying so are
that it contradicts God's nature. Thus it would seem that
ultimately he regards God's nature as the standard. For
example, he writes, "God is the substance of what is possible. . . . Whatever contradicts His own being is impossible
for Him and therefore generally and in the world. . . . But
again it is He and He alone who controls and decides what
manifests Him and is therefore possible, and what contradicts Him and is therefore impossible."[29] Here the standard
is God himself in terms of his being, whereas particular
cases of meeting or failing to meet the standard are decided
by God's will.

What is bothersome about this analysis is Barth's contention that the ultimate standard of possibility is what
"contradicts God." It is not simply God himself who is
the standard, but the contradictory of God's being or will.
But this definition already contains the logical term "contradicts." In short, though God may decide what in particular contradicts him—whatever this may mean, if anything—he does not *decide* that the impossible *contradicts*
him and his nature; the idea that the impossible *contradicts*
his nature seems to be a logically prior concept. As logically
prior, it seems to entail some independence for the standards of logic.

One possible resolution of the difficulty is to say that the
laws of logic are eternal laws in the mind of God. They are
not created by him and thus are not dependent upon his
whim and fancy. God cannot simply make the laws of

logic to be what he wants them to be. Rather, they partake of the character of the necessary being: they can neither come into nor pass out of existence. As governing principles, rooted in his mind, they govern the decisions and actions of God. They function as necessary structures of thought and action—both his and ours. Thus, in their function they are independent of God in that he cannot act contrary to them. Since they are dependent upon his eternal mind for their existence, however, we are freed from the necessity of postulating an ontological dualism, where God is dependent upon some other eternal being or set of laws.

Returning to the question of the status of the moral standard, it would seem that we can say much the same about it as we have just said about the laws of logic. The moral law is eternally in the mind of God. It is not created by him and thus not dependent upon his whim and fancy. He cannot make the moral law to be merely what he wants it to be; goodness by divine fiat cannot be made evil, and vice versa. Rather, the moral law partakes of the character of the necessary being: it can neither come into nor pass out of existence; it is eternally true. As a governing standard, the moral law governs God's actions, but in a way different from the laws of logic. The laws of logic govern God's actions necessarily; he *cannot* perform the self-contradictory. The moral law does not, however, for reasons given above having to do with significant freedom and moral responsibility, govern his actions necessarily. That is, the moral law does not govern him in the sense that the good is the only thing he can do, but rather in the sense that all his actions can be evaluated by this standard.

Thus, in one sense the moral law stands independent of God, that is, in the sense that his acts can be evaluated by it. As a law in the eternal mind of God, however, the moral law is not ontologically separate and independent of God who is the eternal, original reality. The moral law has reality in him, and in effect is instantiated in the world by him in his creative act.

Thus we can reply to the objection raised by Barth, i.e., that in making God's actions subject to moral evaluation we have placed something higher than God and in effect, like Kierkegaard's Cartesian dolls, have stood things on their heads. If the moral standard is in the mind of God, it is not higher than God. The mind of God is still "part" of God and hence not "higher" than God. Indeed, the whole notion of "higher" here is misused. The actions of God are evaluatively subject to the moral law, yet there is no onto-logical dualism, for the moral law is dependent for its ex-istence upon God's eternal mind. Thus there is no implicit ranking involved between the being of God and the moral law which depends for existence upon his mind. The stan-dard of moral evaluation, to which all, including God, are subject, is to be found in God himself—in the eternal, per-fect, moral law in his mind.

A third objection is made regarding our use of the word "praiseworthy" in speaking of God's significantly free ac-tions as measured by the moral law. H. P. Owen writes, "It is absurd to say that when we call God good we are simply expressing our approval of him. He *is* goodness; for in him essence and existence are identical, so that creatures are good to the extent that they mirror him."[30]

Owen is right when he says that to call God good we are doing more than simply expressing our approval of his ac-tions. We are indeed describing an objective feature of his actions and person. We are not simply claiming that his being or actions please us or that we approve of them; we are saying that his actions meet and correspond with the ultimate standard of right and wrong. Thus interpreted, the use of "approved" avoids subjectivism.

On the other hand, to agree here with Owen does not

commit us to his further position that ethical goodness is the essence of God, insofar as it is a necessary structure of his being. We can hold an objectivist position and still maintain that goodness as a personal quality depends on the character of one's intentions and actions. I am good—not merely approved—because my intentions and actions meet an objective standard of right and wrong. Similarly, it would seem, with God, though in his case his relation to the standard differs from ours. The standard of right and wrong would not exist if there were no God, but my non-existence would not affect the existence of the standard.

It might be objected, finally, that to predicate goodness of God with respect to his acts rather than his being is to diminish an essential attribute of his nature, namely, his holiness. Holiness now would seem to become an accidental feature of God, something which he attained, rather than an essential feature of his being. God now *becomes* holy, not *is* holy. But this view of God jeopardizes his worthiness of worship.

This objection, however, reveals a misunderstanding of the term "holiness." As Brunner writes, "It is necessary to consider this word apart from all that has gradually adhered to it, and altered it, in the course of its long history. Originally, the word 'holy' had no ethical connotation. . . . Holiness is the Nature of God, that which distinguishes Him from everything else, the Transcendence of God in His very Nature, as the 'Wholly Other'."[31] Holiness, therefore, is not so much an ethical category as a metaphysical one, one which designates God's uniqueness and his transcendence over all his creation.[32] It includes the transcendence not only of his being, but also of his will. "The concept of 'the Holy' contains the element of Will, and precisely that Will which is set upon proclaiming Himself as the 'Wholly Other'."[33]

CONCLUSION

What we have learned from a comparison of these two answers to the question "Why is God good?" is that what we are involved with in these two views are two different notions of goodness. Goodness can be both a perfection of being and a moral quality. In the former case, as we argued above, it seems devoid of any ethical aspects. Goodness refers to the superb degree to which one has the perfection of ontological qualities and attributes. It is to have "overcome" certain lacks by virtue of the very fact that one exists or exists in a certain way (has certain characteristics). It is in this sense that goodness is predicated of God in virtue of his nature. The second sense predicates good of beings in virtue of their actions, intentions, and dispositions; this use of good invokes the ethical sense. Herein God is good, not necessarily or essentially, but because of what he does, intends, and is disposed to do. And he is perfectly good because he always does, intends, and is disposed to do good acts.

NOTES

1. For the difference between immanent and transient acts, see Francis Nugent, "Immanent Action in St. Thomas and Aristotle," *New Scholasticism* 37, No. 2 (April 1963), 164–87.

2. The implication of this is that the existence of evil lacks falsificatory value for the convinced traditional theist, since empirical data are irrelevant to determining God's goodness.

3. G. Stanley Kane, "The Concept of Divine Goodness and the Problem of Evil," *Religious Studies* 11 (March 1975), 49–71.

4. Thomas Aquinas, *Summa Theologica* I, q.5, a.3.

5. Aquinas, *S. T.*, q.3, a.4.

6. Aquinas, *S. T.*, q.3, a.2.

7. Aquinas, *S. T*, q.4, a.1 and 2. We cannot here develop it, but it is worthy of note that this argument invokes philosophical principles long open to dispute: the doctrine of degrees of being or participation in

being, the identity of God's essence with his existence, and the doctrine that existence is a perfection.

8. Aquinas, *S. T.*, q.6, a.1; q.44, a.4.

9. Aquinas, *S. T.*, q.5, a.4. It is important to note that for the Thomist "goodness is found formally in the thing sought or enjoyed, and not in the appetite that seeks it." Joseph Owens, *An Elementary Christian Metaphysics* (Milwaukee: Bruce, 1963), p. 120.

10. Aquinas, *S. T.*, q.5, a.1. I am grateful to Jorge Gracia for his suggestion to use "coextensive" to understand *in quantum*.

11. Aquinas, *S. T.*, q.19, a.3. According to Thomistic thought, the only act necessary to God is that he seek to promote his own good. God wills (loves) himself as the highest good, and this he does necessarily. All other actions, including his creation of other beings, are voluntary. In creating, he wills things for the good, which is himself. "God wills things apart from himself insofar as they are ordered to His own goodness as their end." The end of creation is the goodness of God. The creation, however, does not add anything to his intrinsic goodness; God, as complete and perfect in himself, cannot have anything added to him.

God loves himself and he does so perfectly, as befits both his own nature and the object of his love. How then does he love us? God loves all things since they are good. But the goodness of things is not intrinsic to them; it comes from God who is the source of their existence. God loves things, not because he needs them, but only on account of his goodness (q.20, a.2, obj.3). As W. R. Matthews puts it in describing the Thomist position: "God loves other beings only insofar as His own perfections are found in them, each in proportion to its value; and, since the different degrees of perfection in finite beings are gifts of God and imitations of His essence, everything in them which God finds worthy of His love is a reflection of His own infinite perfection" (*God in Christian Thought and Experience* [London: Nisbet, 1939], p. 231). See Aquinas, *S. T.*, q.20, a.2–4.

But is this an adequate concept of God and his love? For one thing, are our love of God and our glory to God so worthless that they can add nothing to God? Does not this conception of divine perfection make creation into an insignificant exercise in which God did not have to participate, but did, though all that takes place ultimately has no effect on him? This follows most clearly, I believe, from the Thomistic contention that it is a mistake to see the creation as bringing about a reciprocal relation between God and the creation. For example, Etienne Gilson argues that God's relation to the creation is unilateral, established between the creature and the Creator, and not reciprocal (*The Christian World of St. Thomas Aquinas* [New York: Random House, 1956], p. 128. Aquinas, *S. T.*, q.13, a.7; q.45, a.3). Rather, it seems preferable to hold that "not only does God influence every occasion of experience, but also, he is in turn affected by each. He takes up into himself the whole richness of each experience, synthesizing its values with all the rest and preserving them everlastingly in the immediacy of his own life" (John B. Cobb Jr., *God and the World* [Philadelphia: Westminster, 1974], p. 38). (This thesis is more substantially defended in Charles Hartshorne, *The Divine Relativity* [New Haven: Yale University Press, 1948.])

Secondly, does not this view of God's love run counter to what love should be when it turns God's love for us into self-love? Matthews is correct when he writes, "This is surely very near to a rejection of the belief that God loves the world or human persons at all. On this view, in the proper sense the divine Love is self-love. God loves me only insofar as He finds Himself in me. The world is, as it were, a mirror in which God perceives dimly reflected His own perfection. We must admit that there is an element of truth in the contention that the highest love is necessarily concerned with good; but it can hardly be questioned that this view runs counter to both the New Testament revelation and the noblest expressions of human love. . . . It is precisely because God loved us when we did not deserve it, because while we were yet sinners Christ died for us, that there is any good news of God to proclaim" (pp. 227–28).

12. This is the Augustinian doctrine of impeccability. Not only does God not do evil, but he cannot do evil. Some have failed to see the role this thesis plays in arguments which deal with aspects of divine goodness. For example, G. Stanley Kane (61–62) totally ignores this thesis in his evaluation of what he calls the superior-source responsibility theory.

13. Aquinas, *S. T.*, q.25, a.5, rep. 2.

14. Of course, if the man intended to beat his wife (though unable to carry it out) and the woman intended to injure the other, this would reflect negatively on their moral characters. But this is to introduce another feature, namely, the intentions of the individual.

15. Some writers have raised objections to making God himself the norm or standard of the good. For example, A. C. Ewing argues that if God is held to be the standard of good, either we "expose ourselves to the charge of being guilty of a vicious circle, since we should in that case have defined both God in terms of goodness and goodness in terms of God" (*Prospect for Metaphysics* [London: Allen & Unwin, 1961], p. 41), or we make God's will the standard of all moral conduct, with the result that the right or good is purely arbitrary. "If what was good or bad as well as what ought to be done were fixed by God's will, then there could be no reason whatever for God willing in any particular way. His commands would become purely arbitrary. . . . Since there

was no ethical reason for his commands, God might in that case just as well command us to cheat, torture and murder, and then it would really be our duty to act like this" (Ewing, p. 39). It is not that God does will these actions, but rather that there is no morally sufficient reason for his not willing them, and if he would will them, the very fact that it was God who did the willing would mean that these acts would be good, and indeed, by virtue of the fact that morality is founded upon his will, they would be the standard of our own moral conduct.

Thomas Mayberry also puts the objection in the form of a dilemma. Either God can justify his commands, in which case he must appeal to an independent standard of good, which would contradict the thesis that God himself provides the standard for the good, or else he cannot justify his commands, in which case they are arbitrary (Thomas Mayberry, "Morality and the Deity," *Southwest Journal of Philosophy* 1 [Fall 1970], 122).

But these objections misconceive the position. They seek to separate God's will from its ground in his essential goodness. To the contrary, God's will is identical with and hence inseparable from God's essence. God's nature is good; therefore God cannot will anything inconsistent with the good which he is. Consequently, God's actions and willing are not arbitrary; neither is there any possibility that God would ever condone or will such prima facie immoral actions because he could not, for such actions would be contrary to his very nature. It is true that if God would will such acts they would be the standard of morality. But both the antecedent and the consequent are necessarily false: by his very essence God is precluded from willing anything inconsistent with the good which he is. Thus it would seem that one could slip between the horns of Mayberry's dilemma by arguing that God can justify his commands in terms of his own nature; his commands are good because they follow from his nature, which is goodness itself. And since we have not defined God's goodness in terms of his commands, Ewing's accusation of circularity collapses.

Mayberry might reply by restating his dilemma as follows: either God can justify the goodness of his nature, which would require appealing to an independent standard of good, or else God cannot justify the goodness of his nature, in which case that he is good is arbitrarily decided. This latter dilemma can be escaped, however, not only in the way developed by Aquinas, who gives reasons to show that God is perfectly good, but also by contending that the line of justifications must come to an end somewhere. In saying that God's nature provides the standard of good, the theist implies that it would be meaningless to ask for a moral justification of his nature. It would be like asking why the standard meterstick is a meter in length. At such a point, it is appropriate to reply that it is a meter in length simply because that is what it is.

Similarly, it would seem appropriate to reply that it is just the case that God is good in his nature simply because he is good.

Of course, this reply to the dilemmas—that God's will is grounded on his good nature—depends on the contention that moral good can be predicated meaningfully of the nature of God on the basis of his being. But should this prove meaningless—as we shall argue shortly—this defense collapses.

16. Thomas Aquinas, *On the Power of God*, q.1, a.6, rep.7.

17. The claim that God could choose to do evil must be distinguished from claims which connect the possibility of doing good with weakness of character. Hints of this are to be found in Ninian Smart, when he writes that "the concept *goodness* is applied to beings of a certain sort, beings who are liable to temptations, possess inclinations, have fears, tend to assert themselves and so forth" ("Omnipotence, Evil and Supermen," *Philosophy* 36, No. 137 [1961], 188). Whatever Smart's position, John Hick does draw such a connection. "Smart has shown that a morally untemptable being could not properly be described as good as this term is normally used in ethical discussion. A creature not subject to temptation, or to fear, lust, envy, panic, anxiety, or any other demoralizing condition would no doubt be innocent but could not justifiably be praised as being morally good. In order to possess positive goodness men must be mutable creatures, subject to at least some forms of temptation. This is the valid conclusion of Smart's reasoning" (*Evil and the God of Love* [Glasgow: Collins, 1968], pp. 306–307). J. E. Barnhard ("Omnipotence and Moral Goodness," *The Personalist* 52 [Winter 1971], 107) is right in noting that if such were the case, this would have to be applied to God as well. But would a being subject to lust, envy, panic, anxiety, etc., be worthy of worship?

18. It is interesting to note how Aquinas deals with Aristotle's affirmation that "God can deliberately do what is evil." Aquinas interprets it either as a counterfactual or as a statement about our limited knowledge—it appears evil to us, but really is not evil. *Summa Theologica* I, q.25, a.3, rep.2. For an analysis of the inadequacy of these replies, see Nelson Pike, "Omnipotence and God's Ability to Sin," *The American Philosophical Quarterly* 6, No. 3 (July 1969), 210–14.

19. In many respects, the gospel story of Jesus' temptation in the wilderness points in this direction. The point of the story is well summed up by the author of Hebrews when he writes, "He in every respect has been tempted as we are, yet without sinning" (4:15). The temptations must be seen to have been real temptations to sin. And to be real temptations, there must have been the possibility that Jesus could actually have succumbed to them. It is the fact that he did not yield, and so was without sin, which thus becomes significant. His sinless perfection was not a

necessary consequence of who he was, but of what he did. This is particularly significant insofar as one treats Jesus as a revelation of God.

20. Jonathan Harrison, "Geach on God's Alleged Ability to Do Evil," *Philosophy* 51 (1976), 209, 214–15.

21. Pike, 208.

22. Karl Barth, *Church Dogmatics* II, ii (Edinburgh: Clark, 1957), 521.

23. Barth, 522.

24. Barth, 522–23.

25. Barth, *Church Dogmatics* II, i, 538. This is not to say that the laws of logic limit God's acts. "To do the impossible is impotence" (533).

26. Barth, II, i, 536.

27. Barth, II, i, 535. Kane, 70, in charging an inconsistency in the position of people like Barth, fails to realize that Barth gives similar arguments for the dependence of the laws of logic upon God as for the dependence of the standard of goodness upon God.

28. Barth, II, i, 534.

29. Barth, II, i, 534.

30. "Goodness," *Dictionary of Christian Ethics*, ed. John Macquarrie (London: SCM Press, 1967), p. 138.

31. Emil Brunner, *The Christian Doctrine of God* (London: Lutterworth Press, 1949), p. 158.

32. It should be carefully noted, however, that for Brunner "the Moral is an integral element in the Holy" (p. 166), though this connection was a later revelation. He can say this because he rejects any autonomous standard of right and wrong; the standard is to be found in the will of God. "That which is morally 'good' is identical with that which is determined by the will of God. The only 'good' will is one that wills—utterly and entirely—only what God wills, and one which wills this—simply and utterly—because God wills it. . . . What God wills is the foundation of all true morality" (pp. 166–67).

33. Brunner, p. 159. See also Rudolph Otto, *The Idea of the Holy* (London: Oxford University Press, 1923), chs. 2, 5, and 8.

8

Is God Omnipotent or Finite in Power?

DISCUSSION OF THE PROBLEM OF EVIL generally proceeds under the explicit assumption that the God who is perfectly good is likewise omnipotent. But is God really omnipotent? What is it to be omnipotent? Is it possible to provide an adequate analysis of omnipotence, for example, one which successfully meets the challenge raised by the Paradox of Omnipotence: can an omnipotent being create an object bigger than it can lift? The challenge is not meant to be silly (for it describes a task which we as finite human beings can perform) or picayune, but rather seeks to place in sharper focus the question whether the concept of omnipotence is internally consistent, such that the term can be predicated meaningfully of some being. Perhaps the theist is not necessarily committed to maintaining that God is omnipotent. If God is finite in power, yet greatly more powerful than any other being, this might circumvent or, better, make irrelevant some of the difficulties arising from the doctrine of omnipotence, and most importantly, might provide an easier yet intellectually satisfactory resolution of the problem of reconciling the existence of a good God with human pain and suffering.

On the other hand, if God is finite in power, what constitutes his limits, or what would limit him, particularly if he is considered the creator of all that is? Does appeal to a finite God really provide a satisfactory resolution to the problem of pain? Would a being finite in power be disqualified from being an object of religious worship? It is this bundle of interconnected questions which will occupy our attention in what follows.

WHAT IS OMNIPOTENCE?

Literally, "omnipotent" means "all-powerful." Defined as such, it would appear that

> (A) A being x is omnipotent if and only if it is able to bring about any state of affairs S.

That is, there is no state of affairs that it cannot bring about; or alternatively put, there is no action or task that it cannot perform. This is a commonly held view among those who have not thought extensively about the issue, but it is unsatisfactory, for there are some states of affairs that it is impossible for this—or any being—to bring about, but which inability would not seem to impugn its omnipotence. It cannot bring about the existence of a round square, nor can it *now* bring it about that the past (e.g., that the American Civil War was fought between the North and the South) did not happen. Neither can it bring about the performance of a free act by a free agent (supposing that one adopts an indeterminist view of human freedom). The first is the most obvious, for the property of roundness is logically incompatible with the property of squareness. In the second case, it is contradictory to claim that that which *in fact* happened in the past did not happen. In the third case, for one agent to bring it about that another agent performs an action freely is incompatible with the freedom of that second agent, for that an agent does an act freely means (in part) that it does one thing rather than another and no other agent causes it to do one thing and not the other. A second kind of state of affairs which an omnipotent being cannot bring about is a logically necessary state of affairs (e.g., $7+5=12$; a green thing is a colored thing; a bachelor is an unmarried man). Since these obtain in all possible worlds, one cannot be said meaningfully to have brought about a logically necessary state of affairs; that is, it is contradictory to say that one has brought about that which always obtains.

That an allegedly omnipotent being cannot bring about these states of affairs, however, does not tell against its omnipotence, for in fact these states of affairs cannot be brought about by anyone. For example, with respect to self-contradictory propositions it is not due to any lack of power that they cannot be made true; it is simply logically impossible that a state of affairs should actually obtain which would make these propositions true. When a proposition cannot be made true, either because it is self-contradictory or always true, one cannot fault an agent for not being able to make it true.

Taking both points into consideration, we might modify our definition of omnipotence to read as follows:

(B)   A being x is omnipotent if and only if it is capable of bringing about any contingent state of affairs whose description does not contain or entail a contradiction.

On this definition, counter-cases such as those developed above would not count against the omnipotence of a being. For example, since the description of a square circle is self-contradictory, it is excluded from those states of affairs which an omnipotent being would be expected to be able to bring about. But what about what might be called empirical impossibilities; are these likewise excluded by this definition? Take, for example, the state of affairs S1: "the finding of a man taller than Dan Koehler." On the surface it would seem that the description of this state of affairs is not self-contradictory, for it seems possible that there is a man who is in fact taller than Dan Koehler. But what if there were no taller man? What if Dan Koehler is in fact the tallest man alive? Then no being could bring about this state of affairs. But then failure to bring about this state of affairs is irrelevant to determining the omnipotence of any being. We can show this by our definition, for there is another proposition entailed by the description of state of affairs S1 which is logically self-contradictory, viz., the finding of a man taller than the tallest man alive. In this way empirical impossibilities can likewise be handled by this definition of "omnipotence."

There are, however, some genuine counter-cases to the above definition. Consider, for example, the state of affairs of there being an object which an omnipotent being did not make. The description of this state of affairs is not self-contradictory. This can be seen in the fact that this is a state of affairs that I as a non-omnipotent being can bring about. Yet, though it is a state of affairs that an omnipotent being cannot actualize, this would not count legitimately against a being's being omnipotent, for the description of the state of affairs excludes its being actualized by an omnipotent being. But the exclusion of an agent or class of agents from bringing about a state of affairs hardly is a fair test for whether a being really is omnipotent.

Accordingly, we might revise our above definition to read:

(C) A being x is omnipotent if and only if it is capable of bringing about any contingent state of affairs (*a*) whose description does not contain or entail a contradiction, and (*b*) whose description does not exclude or entail the exclusion of x or any omnipotent agent from among those which may have brought about that state of affairs.[1]

Though this definition seems adequate in that it pro-
hibits the inability to bring about certain states of affairs
which are impossible or unreasonably restrictive from
counting against the omnipotence of a being, it unfortunately has the consequence of being too broad. For example, suppose there is a being who necessarily can perform only one action, like scratching his ear. Let us, for
short, call him McEar.[2] Now since McEar can perform
only one task, he hardly merits being termed omnipotent.
Yet he meets the criteria enumerated in (C).

To see this, consider first the proposition

(1) McEar mows his lawn.

Is there a logically possible state of affairs which could
make this proposition true? The answer is no, for this
proposition contains a contradiction. This can be seen
more easily by replacing the subject term with what it is an
abbreviation for, "a being who necessarily can only scratch
his ear." Thus we have

(2) A being who necessarily can only scratch his ear mows
his lawn.

Since proposition (1) is logically equivalent to (2), and
since (2) contains a contradiction, so does (1). Hence,
(1) fails to meet criterion (a) of our definition (C). Accordingly, the fact that no one can bring about the state
of affairs described in (1) would be irrelevant to determining the omnipotence of any being.

With this background, let us now ask, "Is McEar, understood as necessarily possessing the property of being
able only to scratch his ear, an omnipotent being?"
Consider

(3) For any action A, McEar performs action A,

where A is any act other than scratching his ear. The analysis we gave to (1) likewise applies to (3); since McEar's condition is an essential one, there is no possible state of affairs which could make (3) true; hence (3) fails to meet condition (*a*) of our definition. Consequently, (3) is irrelevant to determining whether McEar is omnipotent. On the other hand,

(4) For any action $\overline{A}$, McEar performs action $\overline{A}$

can be satisfied by McEar. But then it would follow that McEar is omnipotent, for McEar can do the only action he is logically capable of doing. Thus, our definition is too broad, for it can be met by beings which clearly are not omnipotent.

Someone might reply, however, that McEar is not omnipotent because there are some states of affairs that it is logically possible for an agent to bring about which McEar cannot bring about. For example:

(5) Johnson's car won't start.

(5) meets (*a*) in that some agent could bring about a state of affairs which would make (5) true, e.g., by removing his battery. But does (5) meet (*b*)? Since a contingent proposition entails all necessary propositions, it follows that (5) entails the necessary proposition

(6) McEar does not bring it about that Johnson's car won't start.

Then there is a logically possible state of affairs which will make (5) true, but (5) by virtue of entailing (6) excludes McEar from bringing about a state of affairs which would make (5) true. Therefore, (5) fails to meet (*b*) in definition (C). Hence McEar's inability to bring about a state of affairs that would make (5) true, or to generalize, any proposition like (5)—except ones having to do with the scratching of an ear or McEar's ear—does not count against his omnipotence.

What applies to McEar will apply also to any being who has a limited number of ability-properties, all of which it possesses necessarily. Hence, though one might not expect to meet McEar in our world, there is some possible world in which he or, if one thinks such a being would be a logical impossibility on the ground that to be a living being he would have to possess other abilities, his consorts would be actual. It is the mere possibility that these beings exist, along with the fact that they are admitted to be omnipotent according to definition (C), which creates the difficulty. Indeed, by applying an argument similar to that given above, one could show that objects such as rocks, which are necessarily inanimate, are likewise omnipotent on definition (C).

Obviously what is bothersome about allowing McEar and his consorts to be omnipotent is that he clearly is not omnipotent, at least on any ordinary understanding of the term, for he possesses such limited abilities. That is, we can conceive of beings with far greater abilities. Not only must an omnipotent being be able (have the power) to consistently implement its abilities, but its abilities must be such that a being with none greater can be conceived. It is this latter which enables us to exclude McEar and any other such inappropriate candidates.

Therefore, we might define "omnipotence" as follows:

(D)   A being x is omnipotent if and only if (1) it is capable of bringing about any contingent state of affairs (a) whose description does not contain or entail a contradiction, and (b) whose description does not exclude or entail the exclusion of x or any omnipotent agent from among those

which may have brought about that state of affairs, and
(2) no being y greater in power than x can be conceived.

In making omnipotence a term of comparison, condition
(2) creates the difficulty of specifying what it would
mean for one being to be more powerful than another in
general or overall. How one is to incorporate this comparative aspect into a definition of omnipotence in terms of
an agent bringing about states of affairs is not readily
apparent. For example, we might take (D2) to mean that
there is no being y which would be able to bring about a
greater number of states of affairs. But this is ambiguous.
On the one hand, if it means that for a being to be omnipotent there must be no being capable of actualizing more
or a greater number of states of affairs, then it would seem
that this would not strictly be a characteristic resulting
from the omnipotence of the agent, but rather from its du-
ration. The longer an agent existed, the more states of affairs it could bring about; and if it were eternal, it could
actualize an infinite number of states of affairs. Thus,
any agent which was eternal would be able to produce an
infinite number of states of affairs and thus meet condition
(2), for no agent can bring about more than an infinite
number of states of affairs. If McEar were eternal, then
he could scratch his ear an infinite number of times, thus
bringing about an infinite number of temporally ordered
states of affairs. As such he too could meet condition (2).
   On the other hand, if it means that for a being to be
omnipotent there must be no being capable of actualizing
a greater number of states of affairs at any one time, then
again many beings, including many which are finite, would
be capable of meeting this condition in that at any moment
they would be capable of bringing about any one of an infinite number of possible states of affairs. Indeed, this is a

capability which even I possess and which one of McEar's consorts—possessing a greater number of necessary properties—might possess. Consequently, one cannot understand or specify (D2) in terms of bringing about a greater number of states of affairs.

Some might suggest that this difficulty of further specifying what it means for one being to be more powerful than another in general or overall raises the question whether a general definition of omnipotence is possible at all, a suggestion which at least raises the specter of the unintelligibility of the omnipotence thesis. On the other hand, what necessity is there that this aspect of the definition be so specified? It can be reasonably maintained that (D2) is intuitively clear enough and thus does not require further specification. Since I believe that (D) fundamentally is correct, in what follows I shall work with it, leaving open the question whether further specification of (2) is necessary or possible.

THE PARADOX OF OMNIPOTENCE

Some have sought to establish the unintelligibility of omnipotence by appealing to the Paradox of Omnipotence. Does (D) fall prey to the Paradox? We might formulate the paradox as follows. Where x is any being,

(7) Either x can bring about the existence of an object which x cannot lift, or x cannot bring about the existence of an object which x cannot lift.

(8) If x can bring about the existence of an object which x cannot lift, then, necessarily, there is at least one state of affairs which x cannot actualize (namely, the lifting of the object in question).

(9) If x cannot bring about the existence of an object which x cannot lift, then, necessarily, there is at least one state of affairs x cannot actualize (namely, the bringing about of the existence of an object x cannot lift).

(10) Hence, there is at least one state of affairs which x cannot bring about.

(11) If x is an omnipotent being, then x can bring about any state of affairs which meets conditions (1) and (2) in (D).

(12) Therefore, x is not an omnipotent being.[3]

For (12) to follow and hence for the paradox to succeed, it must be shown that the states of affairs described in (7)–(10) meet conditions (1) and (2) of definition (D). If (7)–(10) do satisfy our definition of omnipotence, then our definition falls on bad times: it succumbs to the Paradox of Omnipotence.

To analyze whether the Paradox is successful, let us focus our attention on (8), for as we shall see, what we have to say about (8) will likewise apply to (9). To see whether (8) meets condition (1) of (D), let me first suggest three possible descriptions of the state of affairs indicated in the antecedent of (8) insofar as they relate to (11).

(13) An omnipotent being creates an object bigger than its maker can lift.

(14) God creates an object bigger than its maker can lift.

(15) An object is created bigger than its maker can lift.

Taking (13) first, does (13) meet conditions (1) and (2) of definition (D)? The answer seems to be that it fails to meet (1). This can be seen as follows. The maker of the object referred to in the predicate is the omnipotent being mentioned in the subject of the sentence; further, this being as omnipotent can lift anything. Hence we can reformulate (13) as

(13′) An omnipotent being creates an object bigger than a being which can lift anything can lift.

But (13'), containing a contradiction, describes a logically impossible state of affairs, and hence in failing to meet (1a) lacks any relevance to the question whether any being is omnipotent.

The same analysis will result from the consideration of (14), provided God is considered necessarily omnipotent, for we can substitute for (14)

> (14') A necessarily omnipotent God creates an object bigger than a being which can lift anything can lift.

As with (13'), so likewise (14') fails to meet condition (1a) of (D) and hence is irrelevant to the issue of omnipotence.[4]

What about (15)? Here it depends on the referent of "its maker." If "its maker" refers to a finite being, then it seems that an omnipotent being can indeed bring about a state of affairs which would make (15) true. For example, an omnipotent being might create a beaver and cause it to construct a 25-foot dam of sticks and mud across a stream, a dam which, once constructed, the beaver as the maker would be unable to lift.

We can conclude then that (8) is either irrelevant to the omnipotence of any being, or if relevant—as in one version of (15)—a state of affairs can be brought about to make (15) true. A similar case can be made for (9); if interpreted along the lines of (13) and (14), (9) fails to meet condition (1a) and hence is irrelevant to the issue of omnipotence; if interpreted along the lines of a finite referent—as in one version of (15)—(9) is plainly false: an omnipotent being can bring about the existence of something which its maker cannot lift, as shown above. Thus, proposition (10) does not follow from (8) and (9) and the Paradox of Omnipotence fails.

LIMITS ON GOD'S POWER

The above discussion suggests that there are certain limits to God's power, i.e., the limits of the rational. Though from the perspective of some, such as Karl Barth, even the imposition of this condition restricts God's freedom, yet it can be argued—correctly I think—that to do "the logically impossible" is to do "nothing."[5] Consequently, this stipulation does not really impose a limit on God's power. But are there other limits to God's power? I wish to consider three such candidates in the succeeding sections: (1) self-imposed limits, (2) limits in God's very being (his boundedness), and (3) limits imposed by the creation itself, seen as self-determining actualities or beings. Let us begin with the first.

(1) Can God Limit Himself?

It is generally maintained by theists that God can limit himself in various ways without at the same time sacrificing his omnipotence. In particular, God limits himself in the creation of human persons who possess free will, for if human persons truly are free with respect to a particular state of affairs, then it cannot be the case that God can control them so that they will choose to bring about or will bring about that state of affairs. Put another way, God's causing them to do action A seems to be incompatible with their freely doing A. Thus it might be claimed that in creating persons who perform a very significant number of free acts and who thus might be appropriately termed free persons, God has made things which he subsequently cannot control.

But this, it is sometimes argued, conflicts with God's omnipotence. This can be shown, it is alleged, by constructing a Paradox of Omnipotence.[6]

> (16) Either God can create things which he cannot subsequently control, or he cannot create things he cannot subsequently control.
>
> (17) If God can create things he cannot subsequently control, then it is possible that there exist things he cannot control, and hence he is not omnipotent.
>
> (18) If God cannot create things which he cannot subsequently control, then there is something God cannot do, and hence God is not omnipotent.
>
> (19) ∴ God is not omnipotent.

In short, the contention here is that the self-limitation of God is incompatible with his omnipotence, such that we must sacrifice belief in one or the other. Either God is finite in power and there exist free beings, or he is omnipotent and cannot limit his power without at the same time losing his omnipotence.

To see whether the paradox is successful, let us take a closer look at premiss (17). We might set out the argument given in (17) more fully.

> (a) If God can create things he cannot subsequently control, then it is possible that there exist things he cannot control.
>
> (b) If it is possible that there exist things he cannot control, then God is not omnipotent.
>
> (c) ∴ If God can create things he cannot subsequently control, God is not omnipotent.

The crucial premiss is (b); is there any reason for thinking (b) true? To answer this, let us first inquire what is the nature of these things which God cannot control, i.e., with respect to which he limits himself. The answer is that these are free creatures, beings whose choices and actions in a significant number of cases—and particularly in those cases which are morally significant—are not caused by anything other than the agent's own self. Thus, for example, the argument in (17) would read:

($a*$) If God can create free creatures which he cannot cause to do any free action A, then it is possible that there exist free creatures he cannot cause to do any free action A.

($b*$) If it is possible that there exist free creatures which he cannot cause to do any free action A, God is not omnipotent.

($c*$) ∴ If God can create free creatures which he cannot cause to do any free action A, then God is not omnipotent.

But is the entailment in ($b*$) true? To answer this, let us first look at the state of affairs, described in the antecedent of ($b*$), which allegedly entails that God is not omnipotent. Supposing that there exist free agents, we might describe this state of affairs by the following proposition:

(d) God cannot cause free agent x to perform free action A.

Therefore, it is claimed that if God cannot bring about a state of affairs which makes

(e) God causes free agent x to perform free action A

true, God is not omnipotent.

But does God's inability to bring about the truth of (e) count against his omnipotence? It would seem not, for the state of affairs described—a free agent x being caused by agent y to perform free action A—involves a contradiction. That is, freely performing action A is incompatible with being caused by another agent to perform free action A.[7] As such it fails to meet condition ($1a$) of definition (D) of omnipotence; there is no logically possible state of affairs which could make (d) true. But being unable to bring about a logically impossible state of affairs does not count against anyone's claim to omnipotence. Therefore, since God's inability to bring about (d) does not count against his omnipotence, (b^*) is false. And if (b^*) is false, (17) has not been shown to be true and the Paradox of Omnipotence fails. In sum, there is no reason to think that being able to limit himself is inconsistent with God's omnipotence.

(2) *God as Internally Bounded in Power*

The finitist conception of God's power, which has gained prominence in this century, comes in various permutations. In this section I intend to consider the view which holds that the limits to God's power are within God himself; in the next section I will consider the view that the limits to God's power are in some sense or other external to God.

S. Paul Schilling, one of the recent defenders of the former view, contends that

> four considerations argue persuasively for discarding belief in the absolute sovereignty of God.
> 1. The pain and travail of evolution; the waste and cruelty of the struggle for survival of individuals and species, . . . the long, slow processes of a creation still unfinished suggest not the determinations of unlimited power but the hazardous activity of a God who is proceeding experimentally. . . .
> 2. The phenomena of quantum mechanics, with its disclosures of indeterminacy at the subatomic level; mutation-producing instability and spontaneity in organic life; and the occurrence of events in the physical order marked by randomness, chance, and unpredictable novelty are activities that are not readily attributable to an all-determining divine will or seen as amenable to such.
> 3. The precariousness of human life, threatened . . . by famine, drought, floods . . . ; the seeming purposelessness of

much evil and its failure to contribute to good . . . undermine the claim that an all-powerful Creator ordains all means to his holy ends.

4. . . . the biblical witness, which portrays God's creative and redemptive work as requiring strenuous, sacrificial, continuous effort.[8]

We must, he argues, abandon the concept of a God who is unlimited and absolute in power, a God who can compel anything to conform to his will. God's power is finite, not because he lacks something that another being possesses, but rather because there is no such thing as absolute, unlimited power. "The all-powerfulness of God may be taken to mean that he possesses all the power there is and all he needs to achieve his ends. This need not imply absolute power."[9] "Finiteness of power may itself be ultimate."[10]

In place of a God with absolute power and absolute control over his creation, Schilling sees a God struggling with and alongside his creation.

> God is striving to bring into existence a world in which high values can be increasingly realized; moreover, that through vast toil and suffering, he is accomplishing this purpose. The data of experience also suggest that it is impossible for him to attain his goals without strenuous, long-continued effort. . . . His character—the ultimate nature of reality itself—is such that his creative activity requires arduous, costly, painful effort.[11]

In sum, there is no omnipotent being; God is boundless in love but by his very nature bounded in power. There are many logically possible states of affairs that God wills to bring or come about but cannot bring about.

The finitist conception of God raises three questions. First, if God's power is finite, what is it about God that limits him? The responses by finitists to this are varied. Perhaps the most well-known of modern finitists, E. S.

Brightman, suggested a restricting factor within the eternal nature of God, called "The Given."

> The Given consists of the eternal, uncreated laws of reason and also of equally eternal and uncreated processes of non-rational consciousness which exhibit all the ultimate qualities of sense objects, disorderly impulses and desires, such experiences as pain and suffering, the forms of space and time, and whatever in God is the source of surd evil.[12]

The Given is eternal within God's experience; it is uncreated, no product of any will. In particular, the non-rational aspect of The Given functions as an internal obstacle and limit to his will and knowledge. It restricts his activity; yet God strives to impose order on it, using it, "as far as possible, as an instrument for realizing the ideal good."[13] But his control over this recalcitrant aspect of his being is incomplete, resulting in temporary defeats of his purposes.[14]

Schilling rejects this view as leading inevitably to dualism, which he finds contradicted by the oneness of reality. Rather, he suggests that God is not limited by anything; it is just that God possesses finite power. As finite in power, he experiences "internal boundaries" to his power: "the frontier of his action is constituted by or is intrinsic to his nature as God."[15]

Manifestations of this boundedness—things which exist and events which occur outside the scope of his will and power, such as spontaneity, indeterminacy, and freedom —are found in the evidence listed above. Yet one has to wonder how, on Schilling's view, that which God himself has brought into existence—created nature—can now function outside his power and control, indeed, to an extent which can significantly frustrate God's will. To say that aspects of nature can and do operate independently of God and in successful opposition to his will suggests not only that nature does possess power of its own, but that its power belongs to it independent of its creator. This is particularly puzzling since Schilling writes that God "is the cause, ground and possessor of all the power there is."[16] If all power has its ultimate and present ground in God, how can that derivative power frustrate God's activity against his will? How can there be any power beyond that which has all power, and how could any power work contrary to the very source of its power? Derivative powers could work contrary to God's will if God decides to limit himself and grant such powers, but self-limitation is not germane to this view because it implies that God actually has the power but chooses not to use but rather to curb it. In short, there is a contradiction between Schilling's contention that there are created things which militate against God so as apart from his will to frustrate his will and power, and his contention that God possesses all the power that there is, albeit limited.

Indeed, if the above-marshaled evidence is to count for anything, it would show that God is not the source and ground for all power, that he is limited unwillingly by that which he has created. Once brought into existence, the world turned out to be more than God could handle; it developed a power and will of its own which could frustrate its creator. Thus we find God struggling, as it were, with his unruly child, sometimes winning to accomplish his purposes, sometimes losing, always seeking new methods, directions, perhaps even ruses.

But this brings Schilling back to the very dualism he wanted to avoid. And a puzzling dualism it is, for where does God's "creation" get its separate and independent power if it did not possess it eternally? Thus, either we must return to the suggestion of a dualism within the nature of God, where God struggles to suppress a recalcitrant element in his own nature (as with Brightman), or we must posit an external dualism, for example, along ancient Platonic lines, where God struggles with the formless, eternal matter to bring order out of chaos.

The latter alternative is explicitly metaphysically dualistic and in direct conflict with the Christian concept of God as the creator of all things, the "Maker of heaven and earth." To defend this view one would have to show that the universe either is or contains a necessary being, i.e., a being which if it exists cannot not exist, which is both self-explanatory and the ground for the existence of all contingent beings not created by God. I have argued elsewhere against this contention and refer the reader to that treatment.[17] We shall have more to say about this alternative in the next section.

The former is unsatisfactory in that it posits surd evil within God himself, making the contention that God is perfectly good a contradiction. As John Hick writes, "If the source of surd evil—of sheer, unqualified, unredeemable evil—is part of the Godhead, the Godhead can no longer be described as unreservedly good. It is partly good and partly evil."[18] Brightman's "solution" dispenses not only with God's perfect power, but more radically with his perfect goodness.

Furthermore, on this view God willingly creates a world which he knows will be plagued by surd evil brought about by his nature and his creative act, and which cannot be justified ultimately by any total good. As such, the problem of evil is reintroduced—the very problem which occasioned Brightman's move to a finitist conception of God —for how can a perfectly good God be justified in creating a world which he knows will be plagued by surd evil brought about by his own nature? If the evil in the world is truly surd, no ultimate justification in terms of higher good is possible.

Brightman replies that God is justified in creating such

a world because of the motive of "rational love" which lies behind the creation of values. He writes:

> One may suppose that there lay before God only two alternatives: that of creating other persons whose existence must contain many irrational evils and that of not creating at all. The latter would forfeit all the values in a social universe, and all the possibilities of human existence. The former would lead to the world of society as we experience it. One may well think that a good God would be willing to endure all the added suffering that would be entailed, and to help humanity to endure and control it, rather than to have a universe without human values. Who would deem this choice wrong? Yet it is one thing to say that creation is justified in spite of surd evils entailed by The Given and quite another thing to say [that the evils are] justified by the total outcome.[19]

He rejects the latter thesis on the grounds that it judges the evils in the world to be justifiable and hence calls evil good. Evil, he argues, is evil, and not good.

Evil, of course, is evil; but to say that the evils of the world are justified by greater good is still to see them as evil. It is simply to deny that they are *surd* evils. Evils remain evil, but their existence is justified by the higher goods which make evil possible or necessary. Indeed, as Brightman himself puts it, "To create evils unnecessarily would be monstrous."[20] Consequently, the following dilemma might be posed to Brightman. Either the existence of evil is justified in terms of the higher good of human values and human existence produced and there is no surd evil to be explained and no reason for God to be thought finite, or the existence of evil is unjustified and the goodness of God can be questioned on the grounds that he created a world which he knew would radically experience unjustifiable evil.

Brightman apparently would attack the second horn of the dilemma, arguing that The Given restricts God's knowledge of future contingents, which reduces his moral accountability.[21] But even were this so, this limitation would have to be significant and extensive enough to cover all cases of created, surd evil in order to absolve God. Brightman rightly seems unwilling to constrict God to this radical degree. Consequently, Brightman's adoption of a finitist conception of God leaves the problem of evil unresolved.

Our second question is: If God is finite, will evil or God be victorious in the conflict? Schilling wants to reassure us that God ultimately will triumph.

> In the world we inhabit and the society we belong to, innumerable events can and do occur that are not willed by God and are not subject to his immediate control. Sometimes his utmost effort meets temporary defeat. There is no absolute guarantee of the outcome; yet no defeat is final. God is constantly exploring and finding new ways of advance and creating new possibilities of value. . . . The faith of the New Testament . . . is . . . that we can trust his good will ultimately to prevail.[22]

The picture painted is of a great general with limited but superior forces, sometimes conquering, sometimes suffering defeat. Before the battle is engaged, there is no assurance of victory. Yet the outcome of the war is guaranteed! By what? Schilling suggests that the guarantee is God's good will! But if God's power is not commensurate with his good will, and if his good will is not sufficient to bring about victory in the individual battles, what power does he have to consummate ultimate victory? Indeed, it is not God's will which prevents victory, but the limited power of the struggling God-general.

Schilling goes on to assure us that God has all the power "he needs for the ultimate attainment of his righteous purposes."[23] But rather than being grounds for assurance, an evaluation of his power yields the opposite conclusion. For if God is eternal, he has been waging this battle eternally, engaging in one tactic after another to realize his purposes. If in an infinite amount of time by his will and power he has not achieved victory, he will never achieve victory by his will and power. The struggle will continue indefinitely. Indeed, to suggest an ultimate end to the struggle seems contrary to what Schilling wants to affirm about God; if God is a God of struggle—whose character demands painful effort and whose central motif is the cross—then there can be no peaceful, all-victorious end. Struggle stands at the heart of God's eternal character; the war rages eternally.

Thirdly and finally, if God is finite in power, would this resolve at least in part the problem of evil and suffering? Schilling's contention is not that the finitude of God accounts for all instances of evil, but rather that it accounts for excess, purposeless, surd evil.[24] As an explanation for evil it must be supplemented by other morally sufficient reasons, as, e.g., the free-will defense and the argument from natural laws.

If the problem of evil is posed in a way which invokes the presence of surd evil, or if it is in fact the case that other morally sufficient reasons do not adequately account for all instances of pain and suffering, then it is a reasonable response to suggest that this evil is only something with which a limited being is incapable of dealing or that a surd element in the creator is a sufficient reason for producing surd evil in the world. But even if we concede the rationality of the finitist's response, one must wonder why in light of the alleged overwhelming quantity of surd evil claimed by the finitist the finitist denies the omnipotence of God rather than his perfect goodness. There appears to be a kind of ad–hoc-ness lurking behind this aspect of the finitist's argument.

Yet, I think it must be admitted that opting for a finite God might resolve the problem of evil—*provided* we were willing to limit God's power to the extent that he really could do nothing about any of the innumerable unjustified evils that plague us, and *provided* his knowledge of future contingents is limited so that God truly did not know how bad his creative activity would turn out. But the more ultimately surd or unjustifiable evils are believed to exist or the less satisfactory other justifications for evil are held to be, the more impotent and ignorant God becomes. At the very least it surely gets close to the point where his sovereignty and foreknowledge are called in question and his continuing creative and redemptive powers are doubted. Once this is done, much of the basis for worship of this being must likewise disappear. But until the finitist more specifically delineates the limits of God's power and knowledge and the quantity of unjustifiable evil, more about this issue cannot be said. It is one thing to claim that God is limited in power and knowledge; it is quite another to specify the degree or extent of those limits. In any case, as we have seen, the attempt to say as Schilling does that God's power is limited but that he has all power is unsatisfactory.

(3) *Limits Imposed by Creation*

We have one last alleged fallacy to evaluate, the discussion of which will introduce the view of omnipotence advocated by Process Theology. David Griffin, calling it the "omnipotence fallacy," presents it as follows:[25]

P An omnipotent being can unilaterally bring about any state of affairs that it is logically possible for a being unilaterally to bring about.

R An actual world (i.e., one with a multiplicity of actual beings) devoid of genuine evil[26] is a logically possible state of affairs.

S Therefore, an omnipotent being could unilaterally bring about an actual world devoid of genuine evil.

All traditional theists, Griffin claims, are committed to this argument. Unfortunately, he continues, the argument itself is not formally valid, since it contains an "oscillation between a logically possible action (P,S) and a logically possible state of affairs (R),"[27] thus committing the fallacy of four-terms.

Griffin is correct in noting that the argument commits the fallacy of four-terms, but he incorrectly locates it in the oscillation between a logically possible action and a logically possible state of affairs. We can remove this oscillation by substituting for P and S propositions logically equivalent to them.

P* All states of affairs that it is logically possible for a being unilaterally to bring about are states of affairs on omnipotent being can unilaterally bring about.

R As above.

S* ∴ An actual world devoid of genuine evil is a state of affairs that an omnipotent being can unilaterally bring about.

So presented, it is readily apparent that the formal fallacy does not rest where envisioned by Griffin. The fallacy of four-terms is committed in that whereas P speaks about states of affairs that it is logically possible for a being unilaterally to bring about, R speaks of logically possible states of affairs.

Thus, as Griffin correctly notes, to make the argument valid another premiss—which affirms that all states of affairs that are logically possible are states of affairs that it is logically possible for one being unilaterally to bring about—is necessary. This premiss Griffin labels

> Q   If a state of affairs among a multiplicity of actual beings is logically possible, it is logically possible for one being unilaterally to bring about that state of affairs.

Granted that PQRS is formally valid, is there any reason why the traditional theist who believes that God is omnipotent must accept the argument? Though Griffin explicitly declares that all traditional theists are committed to this argument, it would seem from what we have said above that the answer is negative, for the simple reason that the first proposition (P*) is false. Take, for example, the proposition

> (20)   George freely performed the action of yelling at his dog.

It would seem that the state of affairs of George's freely yelling at his dog is a logically possible state of affairs that a being unilaterally could bring about; it is a state of affairs that George by himself could actualize. At the same time, it is a state of affairs that an omnipotent being (given that George is not omnipotent) could not *unilaterally* bring about, for to do so would be unilaterally to bring about the state of affairs of George's being caused by another being freely to yell at his dog. Since freely bringing about a state of affairs entails that one was not caused by another to bring it about, (20) entails

> (21)   No other being caused George to perform the action of yelling at his dog.

Thus, it is the case that the state of affairs described in (20) fails to meet condition (1*b*) of our definition (D) of omnipotence, for (21) explicitly excludes any being other than non-omnipotent George, including an omnipotent being, from bringing about the state of affairs in question. Consequently, though (20) describes a logically possible state of affairs, it is not the case that an omnipotent being would be able or expected to bring about that state of affairs. Accordingly, proposition P* is false and no theist can be expected to assent to it.

Griffin, however, rejects the argument PQRS for a different (though related) reason; it is instructive to see what argument he presents, for it will provide us with insight into how Process Theology—a theology constructed on a Whiteheadian–Hartshornean world-view—looks at the question of the nature of God's power vis-à-vis the doctrine of omnipotence.

Griffin rejects argument PQRS—and along with it traditional theism—because both (presumedly)—in invoking Q—presuppose the key premiss

X It is possible for one actual being's condition to be completely determined by a being or beings other than itself.[28]

Traditional Christian theism holds that there is a possible world which God could have created in which what was actual was coerced, destined, or efficiently caused to perform whatever actions it performed. That our world is not like this[29] is due to God's self-limitation. God freely limited his power, granting to human persons (alone) the capacity to act freely. The rest of creation is determined to act as it does because of precedent causes following the natural laws which God laid down in his creation and God's subsequent activity.

Process Theology, on the other hand, holds that the world is composed of actual entities or actual occasions, each of which is essentially and necessarily self-determining and self-causing. These are beings which God does not control, not because of any act of divine volition or divine self-limitation, but because of metaphysical necessity—because of what it is to be an actuality. ". . . It is necessarily the case that God cannot completely control the creatures. The metaphysical category behind this necessity is the category of the ultimate, which involves 'creativity,' 'many,' and 'one.' 'Creativity' is a universal feature of actuality. . . . [Indeed,] to be an actuality is to exercise creativity,"[30] to have power, to be a self-determining being. Thus any world which God could have created (or, better, brought out of chaos, since it is the case that there have always been finite actual occasions[31]) would necessarily contain actual occasions or entities which were self-determining (possessive of power). Furthermore, these self-determining entities are not to be restricted to human or animal agents, but include all actualities—the entire continuum from electrons and protrons (which possess minimal spontaneity) and the smallest living cells to complex organisms. . . .[32]

Griffin's argument fundamentally proceeds as follows:

(22) No actual entity is devoid of power.
(23) If an actual entity can be completely determined by another, it must be devoid of power.
(24) ∴ No actual entity can be completely determined by another.

That is, (X) is false.[33]

What does the falsity of (X) tell us about God's power? Griffin argues for what he calls C omnipotence, i.e., "coherent, creationistic omnipotence." Since the actual world —indeed, any actual world—is necessarily composed of self-determining actual occasions or entities which possess and actualize power outside the control of other beings, a being which is perfect in power cannot possess "a monopolistic concentration of power." Power is a relational concept, such that any "delimitation of perfect power requires a discussion of the nature of 'world.' . . . Hence, before drawing implications as to what a being with perfect power could do, the nature of the things upon which power is to be exerted must be considered."[34] Thus, in defining God's power, the power essentially possessed by all actual entities must be taken into consideration. Accordingly, God does not have all the power, but he does possess all the power a being can conceivably possess consistent with there being other actualities. God, as perfect in power, "will enjoy the optimal concentration of efficacy which is compatible with there being other efficacious agents."[35]

What kind of power, then, does God possess? God's power is not the power of coercion "measured by the incapacity to resist on the part of that on which it is wielded."[36] Whereas coercive power or compulsion is employed upon the powerless, persuasion is employed upon those with power. We have seen that all actual occasions are essentially powerful. For God to coerce actual occasions to perform in a certain manner would be to remove them from being actual occasions, which is metaphysically impossible. Therefore, God's power—and corresponding action—cannot be understood in terms of compulsive, deterministic efficient causation. This means that to speak about God unilaterally bringing about states of affairs, as (D) does, is fundamentally mistaken. Rather, his is the power of influence or persuasion: God "exercises the optimum persuasive power in relation to whatever is."[37] That is, God's power must be thought of in terms of final causation, wherein he introduces ideal initial aims and possibilities and richer possibilities of order and complexity for actual occasions to realize, calls forth novelty and through conceptual innovation free thought and free imagination, and ultimately provides for the freedom of moral responsibility. God's power is seen in his calling and persuasion of actual entities to the full realization of their potentialities. "By the way God constitutes himself he calls us to be what we can be and are not. He constitutes himself so as to provide each occasion with an ideal for its self-actualization, and it is in relation to that ideal that each human energy-event forms itself."[38] Thus it is that God lures each and every actual entity to self-realization according to its nature.

Griffin (and Process Theology in general) wants to contend that God is omnipotent (albeit with "C omnipotence") in his persuasive power. But does his analysis of God's omnipotence satisfy the conditions specified in (D)? That it fails to do so appears to follow from Griffin's contention that an omnipotent being cannot in the strict sense (unilaterally) bring about any state of affairs that is logically possible.[39] That is, his view of God's power seems to fail to satisfy condition (D1). But in departing from definition (D), is not Griffin advocating a conception of a finite God —not that of Brightman and Schilling, who hold God's power to be limited by something internal to God, but a finite God whose power is limited by "creation," by the power possessed necessarily and essentially by other actual occasions?

Griffin argues to the contrary, on the grounds that God has all the power that he conceivably could have; no other being could possess more power. Griffin's mentor, Hartshorne, writes, "If power is in principle shared, then the ideal power, though in a sense relative, need not be 'limited' if this means, 'less than the greatest possible'."[40]

We might put Griffin's response this way. His view of God's omnipotence does meet condition (D2), that is, that there be no other being conceivable with greater power.[41] Furthermore, though it seems to fail to meet condition (D1), this is not the case; God's inability unilaterally to effect logically possible states of affairs is due not to any contingent fact, but rather to metaphysical necessity embodied in the very metaphysical structure of actualities.

For an omnipotent being unilaterally to bring about any state of affairs is inconsistent with there being self-determining actualities. Thus, contrary to appearances, Griffin's analysis of God's omnipotence satisfies (D1), for it defines God's omnipotence in terms of his being able to bring about that which is logically possible for a being of unlimited power to bring about. Since for God unilaterally to bring about any state of affairs is inconsistent with there being other actualities, and since other actualities are the only other metaphysical entities there can be, God's inability to bring about unilaterally any states of affairs is due to a logical (and metaphysical) impossibility, and hence as consistent with (D1) does not count against his omnipotence.

Much of the confusion surrounding this position could be cleared up if Griffin would recognize the distinction between the two senses of "actualize" or "bring about" we noted in Chapters 4 and 6. It is the strong sense of actualize which is used by Griffin when he denies that God can unilaterally bring about any logically possible state of affairs on the grounds that this would be inconsistent with the existence of other actual entities. In the weak sense of actualize, God brings it about that something S happens if and only if there is another state of affairs which God has brought about, and God knows that if such a state of affairs is actual, then S will happen (be actual).[42] In this sense God does not directly cause all states of affairs; however, he does bring about some states of affairs which if actual, S is actual. This weak sense of actualize would be consistent with Griffin's appeal to God's persuasive power, wherein God brings about the state of affairs "X is being persuaded by God to do S," God knowing that if this state of affairs is actual, X will do S (though he is not caused by God to do S, but freely responds to the persuasion).

The conformance of Griffin's analysis of God's omnipo-

tence to (D) and his consequential avoidance of finitism
depends upon his contention that the following propositions are necessarily true [for him in virtue of their being
metaphysical principles applicable to all possible worlds].

(f)   There is an actual world.[43]

(g)   To be a world is to contain actual occasions or actual
      entities.[44]

(h)   All actual members of any world are or are composed of
      actual occasions or entities.[45]

(j)   All actual occasions or entities are self-determining
      beings.[46]

(k)   The only power an omnipotent being can have consistent
      with there being self-determining beings is persuasive
      power.[47]

(m) God possesses unlimited persuasive power.

But are these propositions not only true but necessarily
true? (f) is true, but I see no reason to think it is necessarily true. (g) and (j) are held to be true by definition
of "world" and "actual occasion." Whether or not (h) is
true depends upon how one is to interpret "actual entity."
If interpreted to mean "something that exists," then (h)
seems both true and necessarily true albeit tautological.
(h), however, is not understood by Process Theology to
be trivially true; it is informative about the nature of the
actual members of the world, for when "actual entity" is
understood as in (j), (h) then asserts that all actual members of any world are or are composed of powerful, creative, experiencing—recall Griffin's panexperientialism—
beings. But so understood, is (h) true?

For our purposes, however, I wish to focus on (k), for
if (k) is not true, then Griffin's definition fails to meet condition (D2) (for there could then be a being which was
greater in power than a God who only possesses persuasive
power), and if (k) is not *necessarily* true, then it fails to
satisfy condition (D1) (for then in some possible world

there are logically possible states of affairs which some being could unilaterally bring about which would be consistent with there being self-determining beings).

Is, then, (k) true? Or, put another way: Why cannot an omnipotent being exercise both efficient and final causative powers? Why cannot an omnipotent being bring about states of affairs in both the strong and the weak sense? Griffin himself suggests that this is possible when he argues that "to say that an actuality has creativity is to say that it has power. The nature of this creative power is twofold—the power of self-creation and of other creation. In the language of causation, it is the capacity to exercise final causation and efficient causation."[48] But God himself is an actual entity.[49] Thus, it would seem that God likewise would possess *both* creative powers. In other words, a being greater than a being solely possessive of unlimited persuasive powers can be conceived—namely, one possessing both persuasive and coercive powers.

The main defense of (k) by the Process Theologian is a metaphysical one: self-determination and coercion (efficient causation) are mutually exclusive. Where there is creativity, freedom, or spontaneity—as is necessarily the case with all actual occasions—there must be persuasion, not coercion.

But is not the use of both persuasive and coercive powers consistent with creativity, freedom, and spontaneity? Whitehead himself writes, "The doctrine of the philosophy of organism is that, however far the sphere of efficient causation be pushed in the determination of components of a concrescence . . . beyond the determination of these components there always remains the final reaction of the self-creative unity of the universe. This final reaction completes the self-creative act by putting the decisive stamp of creative emphasis upon the determination of efficient cause."[50] It is not one or the other, but "there is mutual

interaction between the coercive and the persuasive. . . .
Factors can be eliminated and modified in both the coercive
power of efficient and the persuasive power of final causation."[51] Even if efficient causation be seen to be coercive
and irresistible, this causative action only affects (certain
of) the inputs, leaving the actual entity by its own self-determination free to sort among the influences. Freedom is
possible in a world characterized by efficient causation
where the individual can choose from between at least two
alternatives, given the same initial segment containing persuasive and/or efficient causes.[52] But then God's possession
and utilization of efficient causation need not mean the end
of freedom or spontaneous action; actual entities have the
capacity to respond not only to his persuasive actions, but
also to factors produced by his efficient causation.

Indeed, were efficient causation incompatible with self-
determination and were (h) and (j) true, as Process Theology claims, there could be only persuasive power in the
world. That is, if efficient causation is incompatible with
the existence of self-determining beings, it follows that
where there are only self-determining actualities there can
be no efficient causation. It would then follow that either
there is no efficient causation in the actual world (which
Process Theology denies) or both efficient and final causation can be effected on self-determining actualities by
other agents, including an omnipotent one [which would
eliminate this defense of (k)].

Thirdly, (k) is defended as follows: "God's action in
the world must be limited to persuasive final causation, or
there will not be a matrix of efficiently caused relativity in
which responsible freedom can be expressed. . . . A metaphysical situation with static laws of nature could not account for the rise of the good which we experience."[53]
But this response presupposes not only that God can act

only in violation of physical laws, but more radically, that actual entities and the natural laws governing them have always existed apart from any divine efficient causal activity. Actual entities are produced by efficient causation from prior actual entities, and so on back in time, without any beginning in time. Not only does this invoke a denial of the traditional Christian notion of creation (which they willingly concede), but more importantly it involves assuming the very point the argument sets out to prove, namely, that there is no divine efficient causal activity. Thus the argument is circular.

In short, unless both (h) and (k) are true, there is good reason to think that, contrary to their claim, Process Theologians have violated the very condition they insist on for God to be omnipotent [viz., (D2)]. There is good reason to doubt the truth of (k) even on the process schema. And if they attempt to deduce (k) from a more general principle governing the incompatibility of efficient causation and self-determining actualities, then either (h–j) is false (interpreting "actual entity" in process fashion) or there is no efficient causation possible. Since both of these consequences appear unacceptable to Process Theology, it is hard to avoid the conclusion that they hold a finitist concept of God: there is a being conceivable with greater power, i.e., one that possesses both efficient and final (persuasive) causal powers.

CONCLUSION

With this in hand, it is time to return to our original issue, which we can formulate in two different ways. First, *must* God be omnipotent? Those who respond affirmatively generally reason that unless God be omnipotent he is not an adequate object of religious worship; omnipotence is a necessary condition for something to merit worship. We might formulate their argument:

(25) A being must be perfect in order to merit worship.
(26) A being which is finite in power is not perfect.
(27) ∴ A being which is finite in power cannot merit worship.
(28) ∴ A being which merits worship must be omnipotent.[54]

Granted that omnipotence is the complement of finitude of power, (27) and (28) follow validly. Is (26) true? Aquinas writes, "We call that perfect which lacks nothing of the mode of its perfection."[55] Being finite in power is to lack something, i.e., the ability to bring about certain logically possible states of affairs which one has not been excluded from bringing about. Therefore, being finite in power would mean that one is not perfect in terms of one's power or ability. We can grant (26) as true.

The critical premiss is (25). On the affirmative side, C. A. Campbell writes,

> . . . [T]he religious attitudes of worship and adoration are difficult to sustain in conjunction with an explicit recognition that the Being to whom they are directed is defective or imperfect in any way whatever. And we can hardly pretend to ourselves that limitation of power is not an imperfection. . . .[56]

On the negative side, Schilling sees a finite, struggling, imperfect God as more in tune with our own religious needs. We can turn more readily to one who has suffered as we now suffer, to one who has undergone struggle, disappointment, and frustration, who knows how we feel because he has experienced likewise.[57]

In short, the affirmative response argues that (27) is true because (25) is true, while the negative response argues that (25) is false because (27) is false.

To resolve the dispute we need a study of the criteria which a being must meet in order to make it an adequate object of religious worship. To suggest that some people actually worship a finite deity or that the higher religions do not is of no help in answering the question, for what people in fact do provides no guidance for determining whether the object of their religious worship merits worship. Neither polls nor anthropology suffices to inform us what constitutes an adequate object of worship.

But what are these criteria? The subject of appropriate criteria would require a major treatise. Let us focus strictly on the criterion of omnipotence. On the one hand, it would seem that what ought to be worshiped should be more powerful than the worshiper. To worship something less than oneself seems demeaning, for since worship involves service ($\lambda\alpha\tau\rho\epsilon\iota\alpha$), the worshiper who was superior in power (and the same thing goes for all perfections) would be obligated to serve the weaker (or less perfect). It can be argued further that it is necessary that the worshiped exceed in power every other actual being (or at least equal in power that which exceeds all others in power), otherwise (all else being equal) we are worshiping a being inferior to another. But from the fact that the object of worship is necessarily more powerful than the worshiper or any other being (all else being equal) it does not follow that it must be omnipotent. Even Hartshorne's statement—"From the worshipfulness belonging by definition to God . . . what really follows is the unsurpassability of God, not his infinity or absoluteness"[58]—is too strong in arguing for unsurpass*ability* rather than being actually unsurpass*ed*. Mere words make it easy to require passage from actually "superior" to "unsurpassable supremacy" to unlimited, "all-comprehensive," absolutely perfect.[59] Yet, what remains to be shown is that only the latter merits worship and not the unsurpassed.

On the other hand, to the pacifist, power or force has no connection at all with merit. Mere power does not call forth service; indeed, in many instances it is the powerless that we are to serve. That which should summon our allegiance is the moral force or perfection which the individual possesses. Worthiness of worship, then, is to be understood in terms of moral perfection, and this entails nothing about the amount of power that a person has or must have, except perhaps that the individual is capable of realizing some of his moral intentions. On this view, then, power or force stands unrelated to meriting worship.

In short, the most that can be derived from the concept of worship is that the worshiped should be unsurpassed in power, not unsurpassable, and the least that worthiness of worship is unconnected with power. In any case, nothing follows with respect to the worshiped's ability to bring about all logically possible states of affairs which it is has not been excluded from bringing about.

We might formulate our issue in a second way: *Is* God omnipotent? An affirmative response which derives this from the supposed necessity of God's omnipotence encounters the difficulty previously mentioned. On the other hand, the fundamental reason for adopting the finitist position—finding a satisfactory resolution to the problem of evil—lacks compelling force. As I argued in Chapters 3 to 5, a believer in divine omnipotence can provide an intellectually satisfactory resolution to the problem of evil. Further, as we have seen above, though the finitist suggestion might resolve the problem of evil, it does so at great cost, severely restricting God's power and knowledge—indeed, to an extent where God becomes roughly comparable to, if not weaker and more ignorant than, humans, for human agents can eliminate gratuitous evils which God has not eliminated.

Determination of whether God is omnipotent requires treating some writings as both authoritative and revelatory, an assumption I will make without defense regarding the biblical writings. Unfortunately, Scripture contains no explicit statement concerning God's omnipotence, nor does it discuss the issue in any philosophical way. Thus, what must be done is to see whether the conception of God espoused in its pages meets the criteria specified in (D). (D1) appears to be affirmed by such biblical statements regarding divine power as "I know you can do all things, and that no purpose of yours can be thwarted"[60] and "Whatever the Lord pleases he does in heaven and on earth, in the seas and all deeps."[61] That Scripture affirms (D2) is less clear. God is revealed as claiming that he alone is God and that there is no other God besides him. For example, "See now that I, even I, am he, and there is no god besides me; I kill and I make alive; I wound and I heal; and there is none that can deliver out of my hand."[62] But as above, this merely affirms that there is—and since God is the eternal I Am, always will be—no being with greater power. What this does not assert is that there is no conceivable being greater in power.

Though Scripture does not assert that there is no conceivable being greater in power, however, it does not assert that there can be such a being either. The context of the utterances is that of an existent comparing himself to other existents or, at least, to other claimants for the title God. None of the gods of the other nations is truly God; Yahweh alone is God. Consequently, the question of God's status vis-à-vis other possible beings remains unconsidered. But one can reasonably extend the comparison made with contemporary claimants to all possible claimants. Not only is there no being other than Yahweh who is God, and not only will there never be such a being, but by extension there can be no such being; no possible claimant could ever be God or equal to him. In short, by a reasonable extension of the context to consider all possible claimants, a just concept of the biblical God would be that not only is there no being like him in power, there can be no such being like him in power. Thus, one can conclude that according to the biblical concept God does meet condition (D2) as well as (D1) and is omnipotent.

NOTES

1. For a similar definition, see George Mavrodes. "Defining Omnipotence," *Philosophical Studies* 32 (1977), 199–200.

2. This illustration was first used by Alvin Plantinga, *God and Other Minds* (Ithaca: Cornell University Press, 1967), p. 170. He was christened "McEar" by Richard LaCroix, "The Impossibility of Defining 'Omnipotence,'" *Philosophical Studies* 32 (1977), 183. That such a being has only one such property is irrelevant to our case; in fact, a more realistic type of case might be constructed in terms of a being with a larger though limited set of necessary properties. I will use this case, however, because it is simpler and is current in the literature.

3. This is a revision of the argument as developed by J. L. Cowan, "The Paradox of Omnipotence Revisited," *Canadian Journal of Philosophy* 3, No. 3 (March 1974), 436.

4. George Mavrodes puts the point: "The dilemma fails because it consists of asking whether God can do a self-contradictory thing. And the reply that He cannot does no damage to the doctrine of omnipotence. . . . On the assumption that God is omnipotent, the phrase 'a stone too heavy for God to lift' becomes self-contradictory. For it becomes 'a stone which cannot be lifted by Him whose power is sufficient for lifting anything.' But the 'thing' described by a self-contradictory phrase is absolutely impossible and hence has nothing to do with the doctrine of omnipotence" ("Some Puzzles Concerning Omnipotence," *Philosophical Review* 72, No. 2 [April 1963], 221–22).

5. Thomas Aquinas, *Summa Theologica* I, q.25, a.3 & 4.

6. J. L. Mackie, "Evil and Omnipotence," *Mind* 64, No. 254 (1955), 210.

7. Given the indeterminist view of freedom this is the case. On the compatibilist view of freedom the paradox itself does not arise.

8. S. Paul Schilling, *God and Human Anguish* (Nashville: Abingdon, 1977), pp. 243–44.

9. Schilling, p. 189.

10. Schilling, p. 245.

11. Schilling, pp. 189–90.

12. E. S. Brightman, *A Philosophy of Religion* (Englewood Cliffs, N.J.: Prentice-Hall, 1940), p. 337.

13. Brightman, p. 338.

14. It is this aspect—the thwarting or hampering of God's will—which according to Brightman makes his position a finitism. According to him, finitism holds that "the will of God faces conditions within the divine experience which that will neither created nor approved" (p. 282; cf. pp. 284, 313–14). Or to put it another way, God cannot do everything that he wills.

15. Schilling, pp. 246–47.

16. Schilling, p. 248.

17. Bruce R. Reichenbach, *The Cosmological Argument: A Reassessment* (Springfield, Ill.: Thomas, 1972), ch. 5.

18. John Hick, *Evil and the God of Love* (Glasgow: Collins, 1968), p. 39.

19. Brightman, pp. 333–34.

20. Brightman, p. 334.

21. Brightman, p. 337. See also E. S. Brightman, *The Problem of God* (New York: Abingdon, 1930), p. 132.

22. Schilling, p. 258. See also Brightman, *Philosophy of Religion*, p. 338: "No defeat or frustration is final; the will of God, partially thwarted by obstacles in the chaotic Given, finds new avenues of advance, and forever moves on in the cosmic creation of new values."

23. Schilling, p. 248.

24. Schilling, p. 248. See Brightman, *Philosophy of Religion*, pp. 336–37.

25. David Griffin, *God, Power, and Evil: A Process Theodicy* (Philadelphia: Westminster, 1976), pp. 263f.

26. By "genuine evil" Griffin means "anything, all things considered, without which the universe would have been better" (p. 22). It is to be contrasted with "only apparent evils," which are evils "compensated for by the goodness to which they contributed." A "genuine evil" is by definition an evil which cannot be justified by the appeal to a higher good, though there might be other grounds of justification, as e.g., it is a logically or metaphysically necessary feature of any possible world. "Only apparent evils" are justified by appeal to a higher good. Griffin's distinction, unfortunately couched in emotive language, reveals a point generally overlooked by the theist and atheist alike. That is, not all evils must be justified in the sense of being shown to be preconditions for a good in order for the theist to make his case. The presence of surd or genuine evil which does not itself lead to or produce any greater good does not entail anything about the existence of God or his lack of certain properties, *so long as* the *possibility* of there being evil is justified as being logically necessary for a greater good.

27. Griffin, p. 264.

28. Griffin, p. 264.

29. In some quarters of orthodox Christianity the above description is held to apply to our present world. For example, Jonathan Edwards (*Freedom of the Will* [Indianapolis: Bobbs-Merrill, 1969], pp. 259–60) writes, "For, as the being of the world is from God, so the circumstances in which it had its being at first, both negative and positive, must be ordered by him, in one of these ways [designedly acting or forbearing to act]; and all the necessary consequences of these circumstances, must be ordered by him. . . . And therefore every event which is the consequence of anything whatsoever, or that is connected with any foregoing thing or circumstance, either positive or negative, as the ground or reason of its existence, must be ordered of God; either by a designed forbearing to operate or interpose. But, as has been proved, all events whatsoever are necessarily connected with something foregoing . . . which is the ground of its existence. It follows therefore, that the whole series of events is thus connected with something in the state of things . . . which is *original* in the series. . . . From whence it follows . . . that he designedly orders all things." The Westminster Confession of Faith (Ch. III, 1), in affirming that "God from all eternity did by the most wise and holy counsel of his own will freely and unchangeably ordain whatsoever comes to pass: yet so as thereby neither is God the author of sin, nor is violence offered to the will of the creatures, nor is the liberty or contingency of second causes taken away, but rather established," seeks to hoe a middle ground.

30. Griffin, p. 276.

31. Griffin, p. 279; Alfred N. Whitehead, *Process and Reality* (New York: Macmillan, 1929), pp. 146–47, 519; John Cobb, *God and the World* (Philadelphia: Westminster, 1969), pp. 91–92.

32. In that each of these actualities can be influenced by another, it has some sort of perfection, a position Griffin calls panexperientialism (p. 248).

33. The critical premiss in Griffin's argument is (22). In its defense Griffin presents two related arguments. (*a*) We do not experience "any actual thing as being devoid of power," and (*b*) "I have direct experience of my experience itself as having some power to determine itself. . . . Accordingly, this provides me with an experiential basis for speaking meaningfully of an *actual* entity which I can then transfer by analogy to other things" (p. 267). The first (*a*) is a bare assertion about the speaker's limited experience and lacks the requisite universality to establish (22) as a necessary truth. The second (*b*) depends upon the validity of arguing by analogy from my experience to that of all actual entities. Since the argument here is identical in form to that which argues by analogy from the existence of my mind to that of other minds, it is fraught with all the same problems which plague the latter. [See Norman Malcolm, "Knowledge of Other Minds," *Journal of Philosophy* 55

(1958), 969–78.] In fact neither argument (*a*) nor argument (*b*) is relevant to Griffin's position, for (*a*) and (*b*) commence from observations of individual experience and at best yield general truths, whereas (22) is held by him to be a metaphysically necessary truth.

34. Griffin, p. 265.

35. Charles Hartshorne, "Omnipotence," *An Encyclopedia of Religion*, ed. Vergilius Ferm (New York: Philosophical Library, 1945), p. 545.

36. Cobb, p. 89.

37. Cobb, p. 90; Griffin, pp. 276f.

38. Cobb, p. 81.

39. Griffin, p. 280.

40. Hartshorne, p. 545.

41. Unfortunately, neither Griffin nor other Process Theologians inform us how to interpret the phrase "greater power" or "conceivably greater power." Thus, the difficulty we encountered in finding an adequate way to interpret and understand this phrase re-emerges in the process view.

42. Alvin Plantinga, "Which Worlds Could God Have Created?" *The Journal of Philosophy* 70, No. 17 (Oct. 11, 1973), 544.

43. Griffin, p. 279; Charles Hartshorne, *The Divine Relativity* (New Haven: Yale University Press, 1948), p. 73.

44. Griffin, pp. 269, 279. See also Lewis S. Ford, "Divine Persuasion and the Triumph of Good," *Process Philosophy and Christian Thought*, edd. Delwin Brown et al. (Indianapolis: Bobbs-Merrill, 1971), p. 290.

45. Griffin, pp. 249, 277; Whitehead, p. 27; Ford, p. 290.

46. Griffin, pp. 248, 266–67, 276–77, 292; Whitehead, pp. 41, 75.

47. Griffin, pp. 280–81; Ford, p. 289; Dalton D. Baldwin, "Evil and Persuasive Power: A Response to Hare and Madden," *Process Studies* 3, No. 4 (Winter 1973), 267.

48. Griffin, p. 277.

49. Whitehead, p. 28.

50. Whitehead, p. 75.

51. Baldwin, 261.

52. Baldwin, 263.

53. Baldwin, 267–68.

54. Griffin, pp. 256–61.

55. Thomas Aquinas, *S. T.*, q.4, a.1.

56. Charles A. Campbell, *On Selfhood and Godhood* (New York: Macmillan, 1957), p. 291.

57. Schilling, p. 264.

58. Charles Hartshorne, "The Idea of a Worshipful Being," *Southern Journal of Philosophy* 2, No. 4 (Winter 1964), 165.

59. J. N. Findlay, "Can God's Existence Be Disproved?" *New Essays*

in Philosophical Theology, edd. Antony Flew and Alasdair MacIntyre (New York: Macmillan, 1955), pp. 51–52.

    60. Job 42:2.

    61. Ps. 135:6. See also Ps. 115:3, Jer. 32:27, Gen. 18:14, and Mt. 19:26.

    62. Deut. 32:39. See also Deut. 4:35, 39; Isa. 43:11, 44:8, 45:5–7.

Index